Literacy
Trios

MATHEMATICAL VOCABULARY

WILLIAM HARTLEY

HOPSCOTCH
EDUCATIONAL PUBLISHING

Contents

© Hopscotch: *Literacy Trios* ▲ Mathematical vocabulary

Introduction

▲ About the series

Literacy Trios is a series of books aimed at developing literacy skills using activities based on useful and relevant Primary Curriculum themes. The unique feature of the series is the provision of three differentiated photocopiable sheets for each activity within the books. This considerably reduces teacher preparation time by enabling the teacher to cater for three different levels of ability for each activity.

▲ About this book

The activities are split into five chapter headings that correspond to the five strand elements to be found in the National Numeracy Strategy. The mathematical vocabulary content of the worksheets broadly corresponds to the recommendations suggested in the Key Vocabulary booklet which accompanies the National Numeracy Strategy document. In addition to the vocabulary element, each worksheet also contains tasks and activities that will help the child to practiSe and reinforce some of the required language skills listed in the National Literacy Strategy. This makes the worksheets extremely flexible and easy to use in either the Numeracy or Literacy Hour. The worksheet headings give some indication of the main literacy skills required by the child in order to successfully complete the sheet.

▲ How to use the book

The book has been designed so that teachers can 'dip into' it and use any of the worksheets that are relevant to classroom work already planned. Alternatively, the teacher can use the activities to plan a whole unit of vocabulary work based on the suggestions to be found in the National Numeracy Strategy yearly teaching programmes and planning grids.

Broadly, the activities could be used across the whole Primary age range in the following way:

▲ Activity sheet 1 – Infant level (P1–3)
▲ Activity sheet 2 – Years 3–4 (P4–5) levels
▲ Activity sheet 3 – Years 5–6 (P6–7) levels

However, as ability levels vary across age and class ranges, it is up to the teacher's discretion to decide on the appropriate activity sheet for individuals in their class.

Alternatively, the activity sheets could be used within one class to cater for the wide range of ability levels often present.

Answers are provided at the back of the book for many of the questions.

Published by Hopscotch Educational Publishing Company Ltd, Althorpe House, Althorpe Street, Leamington Spa CV31 2AU.

© 1999 Hopscotch Educational Publishing

Written by William Hartley
Illustrated by Cathy Gilligan
Cover design by Blade Communications
Cover illustration by Charlotte Whitehouse
Printed by Clintplan, Southam

William Hartley hereby asserts his moral right to be identified as the author of this work in accordance with the Copyright, Designs and Patents Act, 1988.

ISBN 1-902239-38-5

All rights reserved. This book is sold subject to the condition that it shall not, by way of trade or otherwise, be lent, hired out or otherwise circulated without the publisher's prior consent in any form or binding or cover other than that in which it is published and without a similar condition, including this condition, being imposed upon the subsequent purchaser.

No part of this publication may be reproduced, stored in a retrieval system, or transmitted, in any form or by any means, electronic, mechanical, photocopying, recording or otherwise, without the prior permission of the publisher, except where photocopying for educational purposes within the school or other educational establishment that has purchased this book is expressly permitted in the text.

Name _____

Reading and writing numbers

▲ Join each number to its name.

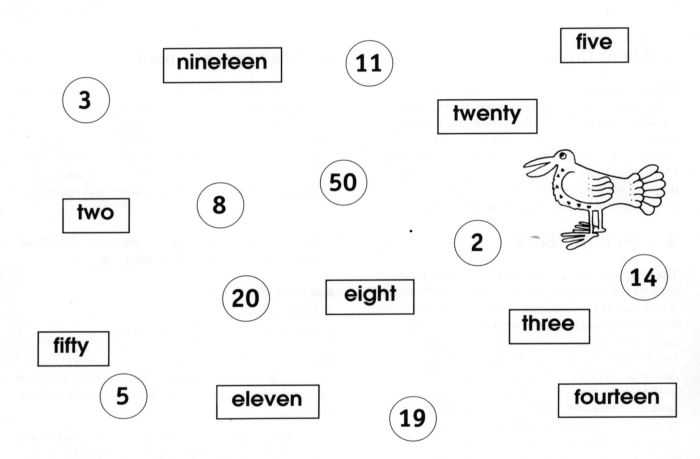

nineteen   11   five

3   twenty

two   8   50

20   eight   2   14

fifty   three

5   eleven   19   fourteen

▲ Write in the missing letters in each of these number names.

o _ e	_ ix	fou _
s _ v _ n	_ en	ni _ e
fi _ tee _	se _ en _ een	thirt _ _ n
si _ tee _	t _ elv _	ei _ _ teen

   © Hopscotch: *Literacy Trios* ▲ Mathematical vocabulary

Name _____

Reading and writing numbers

▲ Join each number to its name.

1000	one thousand and ten
1100	one thousand
1010	one thousand and one
1001	one thousand, one hundred

six thousand, two hundred and twenty	5206
five thousand and twenty-two	6502
six thousand, five hundred and two	6220
five thousand, two hundred and six	5022

▲ Cross out the amounts that are less than two thousand and twenty.

two thousand and twenty-six   two thousand and two

two thousand and twenty-four   two thousand and twelve

two thousand, two hundred   two thousand and twenty-one

▲ Cross out the amounts that are more than three thousand and forty.

three thousand, four hundred   three thousand and four

four thousand and four   four thousand and thirty

three thousand and thirty-nine   three thousand and forty-one

Name _____

Reading and writing numbers

▲ Write each of these numbers as figures.

1. One thousand and five _____

2. One thousand, five hundred _____

3. One thousand and fifty _____

4. Twenty thousand and six _____

5. Twenty thousand and sixty _____

6. Twenty-six thousand _____

7. Twenty thousand, six hundred _____

8. Three hundred thousand and eight _____

9. Three hundred and eight thousand _____

10. Three hundred thousand, eight hundred _____

11. Three hundred and eighty thousand _____

12. Three hundred thousand and eighty _____

13. One million _____

14. One million, seven hundred thousand _____

15. One million, seven hundred _____

16. One million and seven _____

▲ Work out these calculations and write the answers in words.

1. 7404 − 2539 = _____

2. 9472 + 11907 = _____

3. 30251 x 2 = _____

4. 102016 ÷ 2 = _____

▲ Write a number in words that uses all the digits below.

2   5   8   4   3

_____

© Hopscotch: *Literacy Trios* ▲ Mathematical vocabulary

Name _____

Alphabetical order

▲ The words below are all to do with counting.
Put them in alphabetical order.

number   **even**   **zero**   **tally**   **odd**   **pattern**

_____

▲ Choose from the list below to finish these sentences
with the best ending.

1. A **number** is a _____

2. **Zero** is _____

3. A **tally** is _____

4. A **pattern** is a _____

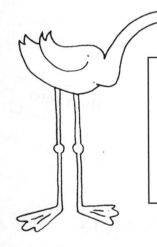

marks to show a score.

layout of numbers obeying some rule.

word or figure showing how many.

shown by the figure 0.

▲ Write the letters of these words in alphabetical order.
One has been done for you.

number	**zero**	**tally**	**pattern**
										a	l	l	t	y								

Name _____

Alphabetical order

▲ Read these words and then put them in alphabetical order.

between   **positive**   **minus**   **negative**   **factor**

exact   **approximate**   **compare**   **unit**   **represent**

_____

_____

▲ Complete each of these sentences with the most suitable ending chosen from the boxes below.

1. **Between** means_____

2. A **negative** amount is a _____

3. A **positive** amount is a _____

4. To **approximate** is to give an answer that is _____

quantity greater than zero

in the middle of

nearly correct

quantity less than zero

▲ Write the letters of these words in alphabetical order.

between   **negative**   **approximate**

▲ On the back of this sheet, arrange these words alphabetically and then write out the meanings of each. Use a dictionary to help you.

minus   **factor**   **exact**   **unit**   **represent**

© Hopscotch: *Literacy Trios* ▲ Mathematical vocabulary

Name _____

Alphabetical order

▲ Write the letters for each of these words in alphabetical order in the boxes.
If the same letter occurs twice in a word record the letter only once in the box.
The first word has been done for you.

1. exchange

a	c	e	g	h	n	x

2. numeral

3. approximate

4. ascend

5. descend

6. estimate

7. exact

8. integer

9. positive

10. predict

11. continue

12. negative

▲ Complete each of these sentences using a suitable ending.
Use a dictionary or other reference material to assist you.

1. A *numeral* is _____

2. To *exchange* is to _____

3. To *estimate* is to _____

4. To *predict* is to say _____

5. To *continue* is to _____

▲ On the back of this sheet, write out the words above that are in italics.
Then arrange the letters of each word alphabetically.

Name _____

Finding and making words

▲ Many words have little words inside them. Look at these words.

none   The word 'none' has <u>no</u> and <u>one</u> in it.

tiny   The word 'tiny' has <u>in</u> and <u>tin</u> in it.

▲ Now look at these words. Underneath each one write 2 little words you can find in it.

start	**before**	**think**	**tally**
_____	_____	_____	_____
_____	_____	_____	_____

pattern	**repeat**	**greatest**	**continue**
_____	_____	_____	_____
_____	_____	_____	_____

▲ In each case below, join the groups of letters together to form a word. Look at your words and next to each one write down as many small words as you can find in it. The first one has been done for you.

lit, sp _split, lit, it_____   **take, mis** _____

le, who _____   **ty, twen** _____

Name _____

Finding and making words

▲ Many words have small words inside them. Look at these words.

position The word 'position' has <u>sit</u>, <u>it</u> and <u>on</u> in it.

exchange The word 'exchange' has <u>change</u>, <u>hang</u> and <u>an</u> in it.

▲ Study these words. In the box underneath each one write at least two small words you can find in it. Don't count 'a' as a separate word.

more	incorrect	record	estimate	place

fraction	sixteen	arrange	calculate	represent

▲ Join the groups of letters together to form a word. Look at your words and next to each one write down as many small words as you can find in it. The first one has been done for you.

cribe, des _____describe_____   **i, fy, class** _____

scribe, rib, be, crib   _____

er, prop, ty _____   **ber, re, mem** _____

_____   _____

© Hopscotch: *Literacy Trios* ▲ Mathematical vocabulary

11

Name _____

Finding and making words

▲ Many words have smaller words inside them. Look at these examples.

factor has <u>fact</u>, <u>act</u>, <u>actor</u>, <u>to</u> and <u>or</u> in it.   **ascending** has <u>as</u>, <u>in</u>, <u>end</u> and <u>ending</u> in it.

▲ Study the words below and then write down as many small words as you can find in each word. Do not include 'a' as a separate word.

1. seventeenth _____

2. smallest _____

3. investigate _____

4. approximately _____

5. interrogate _____

6. adjusting _____

7. factorise _____

8. equivalent _____

9. statement _____

10. rearrange _____

11. separate _____

12. divisibility _____

13. denominator _____

14. reasoning _____

▲ Find two more small words to add to each list below.

proportion	**million**	**thousand**	**relationship**	**nearest**
<u>or</u>	<u>on</u>	<u>an</u>	<u>hip</u>	<u>hear</u>
<u>prop</u>	<u>mill</u>	<u>and</u>	<u>at</u>	<u>rest</u>
_____	_____	_____	_____	_____
_____	_____	_____	_____	_____

▲ Write out eight words that can be made from these word beginnings and endings.

quence	hun	com	bol	correct	pre	pare	dis
dict	com	sym	cuss	se	dred	plete	in

_____

_____

© Hopscotch: *Literacy Trios* ▲ Mathematical vocabulary

Name _____

Jumbled sentences

▲ In brackets are the parts of a sentence. Put the parts in the correct order to make a complete sentence.

1. (is called) (A sign for a number) (a figure.)

   _____

2. (big in size.) (object is) (A large)

   _____

3. (A number) (showing how many.) (is a word or figure)

   _____

4. (whole number.) (the smallest) (One is)

   _____

▲ Draw a pencil line to connect the first half of each sentence with its ending.

The total of something	correct in every way.
Ninety is equal to	that has a meaning.
Exact means	nine times ten.
To check is to make sure	is called the amount.
A sign is something	that something is right.

Name _____

Jumbled sentences

▲ Write out each of these groups of words in the correct order to make a complete sentence.

1. (four hundred.) (is one hundred more than) (Five hundred)

_____

2. (is one hundred less than) (Six hundred) (seven hundred.)

_____

3. (one hundred) (Two hundred) (and three hundred.)

(is halfway between) _____

_____

4. (is to guess) (if the answer is correct.) (without checking)

(To estimate) _____

_____

▲ Draw a line to connect the first half of each sentence with its ending.

A pattern is a layout of numbers	hundred is ten.
To see how alike or unlike things are	makes a pair.
One tenth of a	you compare them.
Two of something	obeying some rule.

▲ Rearrange these words into a mathematical fact. Write your answer on the back of this sheet.

by Ten hundred multiplied ten one equals

Name _____

Jumbled sentences

▲ Sort the parts of each sentence into the correct order and then show the order on the chart by using the letters as a code. The first one is done for you.

1. (multiple of)ᵃ (and fifty-six)ᵇ (Fourteen is a)ᶜ (both twenty-eight)ᵈ

2. (is fourteen thousand)ᵃ (rounded to)ᵇ (the nearest thousand)ᶜ
(Thirteen thousand, eight hundred)ᵈ

3. (Ascending numbers)ᵃ (get smaller and smaller)ᵇ (but)ᶜ
(get larger and larger)ᵈ (descending numbers)ᵉ

4. (of a proper fraction)ᵃ (the denominator)ᵇ (The numerator)ᶜ (is less than)ᵈ

1.	c	a	d	b
2.				
3.				
4.				

▲ Rearrange the jumbled words in these mathematical definitions. One is done for you.

percentage – way fraction another or of decimal writing a

percentage – *another way of writing a fraction or decimal* _____

exchange – one for thing to another change

exchange – _____

consecutive – continuously order following unbroken in

consecutive – _____

property – quality of a characteristic something or

property – _____

▲ The words in the boxes below are jumbled up. On the back of this sheet, rearrange the ones on the left to make the beginning of a sentence. Do the same with the words on the right to make the endings. Draw lines to match each beginning with its ending.

A sequence that belong is a set of things	a certain number that represents
To classify is to items	next to each particular order other in a
A numeral symbol is a	systematically into groups arrange them

Name _____

Questions

▲ Write the answer to each question using a full sentence.

1. How many twos in fourteen?

   There are _____

2. Is twelve more or less than eleven?

   Twelve is _____

3. What is the total of six and eight?

   The total of _____

4. Is fifteen smaller than or greater than twenty?

   Fifteen is _____

▲ Answer these questions.

1. What does the five stand for in fifty-nine?

2. How much is the digit 1 worth in 152?

3. What is five fewer than fifteen?

4. How many do you have if you have double eight?

5. Thirty plus twenty-six is equal to how many?

6. Ten more than thirty-two is how many?

© Hopscotch: *Literacy Trios* ▲ Mathematical vocabulary

Name _____

Questions

▲ Answer the questions below by writing 'Yes' or 'No'.

1. Is four thousand and fifty-six larger than four thousand and sixty-five? _____

2. Is eight thousand and twenty-five more than eight thousand, two hundred and fifty? _____

3. Is seventeen hundred and sixty-five as many as fifteen hundred and sixty-seven? _____

4. Is six thousand, two hundred and fifty-two smaller than six thousand, two hundred and twenty-five? _____

5. Is two thousand and two fewer than two thousand and twenty? _____

▲ Do your working out for these questions on another sheet of paper.

1. Increase thirty-nine by twenty-seven. _____

2. Seventy is how many more than thirty? _____

3. Write down five multiples of six. _____

4. What number is a twentieth of a hundred? _____

5. If forty-eight is split into six equal parts how many will there be in each part? _____

▲ On the back of this sheet, write down the meaning of each of these words.

fraction   quarter   predict   minus   plus   exact

Name _____

Questions

▲ Answer these questions. They all contain words to do with either fractions, decimals or percentages. Use another sheet of paper for any working out you need to do.

1. Divide three hundred and sixty into ten equal parts. _____

2. Show three-quarters as a percentage using the percentage sign. _____

3. Write down three different examples of a mixed fraction. _____ _____ _____

4. Circle the amounts that are proper fractions: $\frac{1}{2}$ $\frac{4}{5}$ $\frac{7}{4}$ $\frac{2}{3}$ $\frac{12}{10}$ $\frac{4}{3}$

5. Show four and seven-tenths as a decimal. _____

6. Ring the amounts that are improper fractions:

   three-quarters   six-fifths   nine-sixths   seven-eighths   nine-thirds

7. Write down two different pairs of equivalent fractions. _____ _____ _____ _____

8. Work out twenty-five per cent of five hundred. _____

▲ Do your working out for these on another sheet of paper.

1. What number is eighty-seven more than nineteen add thirty-seven? _____

2. Forty-seven less than four hundred is how many? _____

3. Ninety-seven is a sixth of what number? _____

4. A threefold increase of eight gives how many? _____

5. Make eight thousand, six hundred and thirty-four smaller by

   one thousand, eight hundred and twenty-five. _____

6. An eighth of nine thousand, nine hundred and ninety-two is how many? _____

7. Make six hundred and eighty-five add seven greater by forty-nine. _____

▲ On the back of this sheet, write down the mathematical meaning of each of these words.

equivalent   formula   property   integer   compare   exchange

© Hopscotch: *Literacy Trios* ▲ Mathematical vocabulary

Name _____

The correct spelling

▲ Write down these figues as words. Use a dictionary to help you. The first one has been done.

1	*one*		2			3			4	

5			6			7			8	

▲ Choose the correct spelling for each number below. Write it in the box. The first one has been done for you.

11	eleveen
	eleven
	elefen
	eleven

12	telve
	twelver
	twelve

13	therteen
	thirteen
	fertean

14	fourteen
	forteen
	fortean

15	fifteen
	fiften
	fitfeen

16	sixten
	sixteen
	sixtene

17	sefenteen
	sevtenn
	seventeen

18	ateteen
	eighteen
	eateen

19	nintean
	ninetan
	nineteen

20	twenty
	twenti
	twentee

30	tertey
	thirty
	thertie

40	fourty
	forety
	forty

© Hopscotch: *Literacy Trios* ▲ Mathematical vocabulary

19

Name _____

The correct spelling

▲ Write down these numbers in words. Make sure that you spell the words correctly. Use a dictionary to help you. The first one has been done for you.

50	*fifty*

100	

1000	

10 000	

100 000	

1 000 000	

▲ These mathematical words have spelling mistakes. Use a dictionary to help you find the mistakes and then write out each word correctly.

decemal	fractoin	twentyeth	quartar
_____	_____	_____	_____

relashionship	preedict	continnu	consekutive
_____	_____	_____	_____

diget	possitive	neggative	aproximate
_____	_____	_____	_____

▲ On the reverse side of this sheet, write out each of these sentences with all the words spelled correctly.

1. Ninety-six is a multipel of both twellve and eigtht.

2. A desimal point seperates hole ammounts from frational quontityes.

3. Seventy-to is twise as larje as theirty-six.

© Hopscotch: *Literacy Trios* ▲ Mathematical vocabulary

Name _____

The correct spelling

▲ Write in the missing letters in each of these mathematical words.
Check your answers with a dictionary.

| c | | n | c | e | l |

| a | p | | r | o | x | | m | a | t | | l | y |

| n | i | n | | h |

| r | o | | g | | l | y |

| d | i | | i | s | i | b | | l | i | | y |

| n | | a | l | y |

| | r | a | c | t | i | | n |

| f | o | | m | | l | a |

| t | w | | l | | t | h |

| e | q | u | | v | | l | e | | t |

| h | | n | d | r | | d | t | h |

| p | e | | c | e | n | t | | g |

| | u | m | | r | a | t | | r |

| | e | s | c | e | n | d | i | | g |

| a | | c | e | n | | | n | g |

| t | h | | u | s | | n | d | | h |

| d | e | n | | m | i | | a | t | o | |

| | e | c | i | | a | l |

| | e | g | h | | h |

| c | | n | s | | c | u | t | | v | e |

▲ Arrange each group of letters to spell a mathematical word.

| gre est at | all sm est | re fo be | twe be en |
| _____ | _____ | _____ | _____ |

| ate es tim | tly ex ac | ar ne est | po ve siti |
| _____ | _____ | _____ | _____ |

| tive ga ne | tte pa rn | vest in igate | fy ju sti |
| _____ | _____ | _____ | _____ |

▲ Choose one group of letters from each of the twelve words in the exercise
above and use that group as part of a new word. For example, the letters
'gre' could be used in the words 'grebe' or 'congregate', the letters 'est' in
'best' or 'chest' and the letters 'at' in 'chat' or 'thatch'.

▲ Write out your list of words on the back of this sheet .

Name _____

Find the synonym

▲ Look for ten words on the monitor screen that have the same meaning as the words in the list. Circle and connect the words together as shown.

To help you the first letter of each word on the screen has been written as a capital letter and shaded.

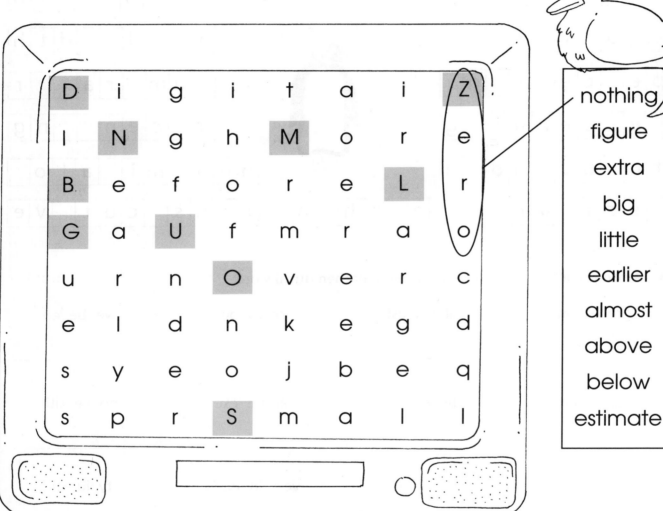

D	i	g	i	t	a	i	Z
I	N	g	h	M	o	r	e
B	e	f	o	r	e	L	r
G	a	U	f	m	r	a	o
u	r	n	O	v	e	r	c
e	l	d	n	k	e	g	d
s	y	e	o	j	b	e	q
s	p	r	S	m	a	l	l

nothing
figure
extra
big
little
earlier
almost
above
below
estimate

▲ Write down any other words you can find on the screen.

_____

_____

© Hopscotch: *Literacy Trios* ▲ Mathematical vocabulary

Name _____

Find the synonym

▲ Look for 12 words on the monitor screen which have the same or nearly the same meaning as the words in the list. Circle and connect the words together as shown. Search in all directions except diagonally. To help you, the start letter of each word on the screen is a capital letter.

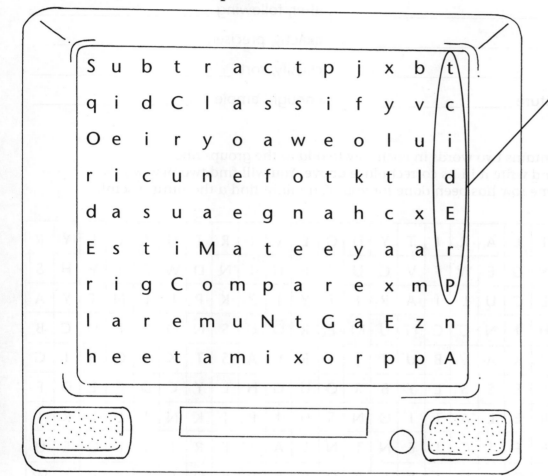

S	u	b	t	r	a	c	t	p	j	x	b	t
q	i	d	C	l	a	s	s	i	f	y	v	c
O	e	i	r	y	o	a	w	e	o	l	u	i
r	i	c	u	n	e	f	o	t	k	t	l	d
d	a	s	u	a	e	g	n	a	h	c	x	E
E	s	t	i	M	a	t	e	e	y	a	a	r
r	i	g	C	o	m	p	a	r	e	x	m	P
l	a	r	e	m	u	N	t	G	a	E	z	n
h	e	e	t	a	m	i	x	o	r	p	p	A

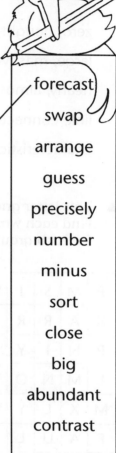

forecast
swap
arrange
guess
precisely
number
minus
sort
close
big
abundant
contrast

▲ Write down any other words you can find written on the wordsearch. You may search for the words in all directions including diagonally.

_____

_____

_____

▲ On the back of this sheet write out the 12 capital letters shown on the monitor screen and use them to make as many words of four letters or more as you can. Use a dictionary or thesaurus to help you.

Find the synonym

▲ A synonym is a word that has the same or a similar meaning to another word. Below are ten groups of synonyms to look at before you move on to the next section.

zero, nought *nothing* _____

large, massive _____

nearly, almost _____

link, connection _____

characteristic, feature _____

many, abundant *numerous* _____

after, following _____

exactly, precisely _____

classify, sort _____

enough, ample _____

▲ This letter grid contains two words in each row to add to the groups above. Find each word and write it in its correct place above. You will find two new words for each group. One row has been done for you. You might find a thesaurus useful.

P	M	S	I	M	I	L	A	R	I	T	Y	D	Q	E	V	I	R	T	U	A	L	L	Y	R
X	A	R	R	A	N	G	E	W	F	V	G	U	B	E	H	I	N	D	W	Z	T	V	H	S
P	N	I	Y	P	E	C	U	L	I	A	R	I	T	Y	J	Z	K	P	L	E	N	T	Y	A
L	M	N	O	T	H	I	N	G	C	N	U	M	E	R	O	U	S	N	O	B	P	D	C	B
M	X	L	Y	W	Z	K	A	V	B	U	T	J	S	R	V	A	S	T	X	I	Q	B	I	G
F	A	U	L	T	L	E	S	S	L	Y	B	R	O	U	G	H	L	Y	C	D	C	E	D	F
N	G	L	H	I	R	E	L	A	T	I	O	N	S	H	I	P	J	K	N	I	L	F	K	J
L	M	S	S	U	F	F	I	C	I	E	N	T	N	L	A	T	E	R	T	Y	F	O	E	U
Q	P	R	A	B	S	O	L	U	T	E	L	Y	Q	R	S	P	R	O	F	U	S	E	T	W
O	P	R	O	P	E	R	T	Y	X	C	A	T	E	G	O	R	I	Z	E	H	G	G	Y	H

▲ Write down another word with a similar meaning to accompany each of these words.

under _____   small _____   plus _____

near _____   pattern _____   minus _____

before _____   digit _____   between _____

last _____   compare _____   size _____

© Hopscotch: *Literacy Trios* ▲ Mathematical vocabulary

Name _____

Do you know?

▲ Read these number riddles and work out the correct answers.

1. Add four to this number and you get eight. ☐

2. Take away five from this number and you have two. ☐

3. This number is one hundred more than fifty. ☐

4. When you share seventeen by five you
   have this number left over. ☐

5. Halve this number and you have three. ☐

6. This number is ten fewer than twenty-seven. ☐

7. Sixteen is twice the size of this number. ☐

▲ Write the answers to these riddles in words.

1. This number is the same as 12 plus 8. _____

2. This number is the same as 14 minus 9. _____

3. 5 lots of 3 equal this number. _____

4. 3 times this number will give you 27. _____

5. This number is less than 5 and a multiple of 9. _____

6. Half of this number is 3 times 4. _____

Name _____

Do you know?

▲ Read these number riddles and work out the correct answers.

1. This number is the remainder when 57 is shared by 4. ☐

2. Subtract 23 from this number and you are left with seventeen. ☐

3. When this amount is shared equally among six people each person gets five items. ☐

4. This number is less than twenty, more than ten and divisible by 2, 4 and 8. ☐

▲ Match the words in the box with their meanings.

twice	half	row	subtract	column	once

1. This word means 'a list of numbers going down a page'. _____

2. This word means 'a list of numbers going across a page'. _____

3. This word means 'one time only'. _____

4. This word means 'two times only'. _____

5. This word means 'take something away'. _____

6. This word means 'one of two equal parts of something'. _____

▲ On the back of this sheet, write down the mathematical meaning of each of the following words. Use a dictionary to help you.

increase	decrease	factor	share	double

© Hopscotch: *Literacy Trios* ▲ Mathematical vocabulary

Name _____

Do you know?

▲ Calculate the correct answers to these number riddles.

1. This number is the remainder when six hundred and eight is divided by six. ☐

2. The number you need to find is a third of four hundred and eighty-three. ☐

3. The total of two hundred and seventy and this number will give five hundred and forty. ☐

4. This amount is the product of nine and twenty. ☐

5. To find this number you must share one hundred and twenty by six. ☐

6. The number I am thinking of is less than thirty, more than fifteen and divisible by 2, 4, 6, 8 and 12. ☐

▲ Join each word to its meaning. Use a dictionary to help you. The first one is done for you.

double	make or become greater
memory	make something a number of times bigger
column	two times only
decrease	a number that will share into another number with no remainder
multiple	the result obtained when one amount is divided by another
quotient	a list of numbers going down a page
increase	make or become smaller
multiply	the part of a computer that stores data electronically

▲ Which two words come next in these number sequences?

seven   twelve   eleven   sixteen   fifteen   _____   _____

three   seven   twelve   sixteen   twenty-one   _____   _____

Name _____

Using a glossary

add	*put things together to make more*
double	*twice the number*
halve	*divide into two equal parts*
once	*one time only*
score	*record of points made in a game*
subtract	*take something away*
total	*all of something*
more	*greater amount*
row	*list of numbers going across a page*

▲ Choose a word from the list to put in each sentence.

1. If you eat _____ the amount you eat twice as much.

2. I _____ went to Scotland for my holiday.

3. Red team had a _____ of twenty in the rounders game.

4. John wrote a _____ of numbers in his notebook.

5. Susan was told to _____ four from her answer.

6. Mum asked Kara if she wanted any _____ biscuits.

▲ Which three words haven't you used in the sentences? On the back of this sheet, write three sentences to show the meaning of those three words.

© Hopscotch: *Literacy Trios* ▲ Mathematical vocabulary

Name _____

Using a glossary

array	*to arrange in order*
column	*list of numbers going down a page*
divide	*cut into parts*
double	*twice the amount*
inverse	*an action that is the exact opposite of another*
minus	*to take away*
multiple	*a number that will share into another number with no remainder*
multiply	*make something a number of times larger*
product	*the answer to a multiplication sum*
repeat	*say or do again*

▲ Choose the most suitable word from the glossary to put in each sentence.

1. Sarah had an _____ of dolls in her bedroom.

2. Ian was asked to find the _____ of six and five.

3. The numbers were written in a _____ in Sue's notebook.

4. Jack was asked to _____ the cake among eight people.

5. Addition is the _____ of subtraction.

▲ Join the words with similar meanings.

group	add	subtract	share

plus	divide	minus	set

▲ On the back of this sheet, write five separate sentences to show the meanings of each of these words.

double   multiply   minus   multiple   repeat

Calculations

Using a glossary

arrange	*to put things in order*
calculator	*an electronic machine for performing mathematical calculations*
column	*list of numbers going down a page*
difference	*the amount or degree of unlikeness*
display	*the numbers that appear on a calculator read-out*
factor	*a number that divides exactly into another number*
identical	*exactly the same*
inverse	*an action that is the exact opposite of another*
multiply	*make something a number of times larger*
product	*the answer to a multiplication calculation*
quotient	*the answer to a division calculation*
remainder	*the number left over after completing a division calculation*

▲ Choose the most suitable word from the glossary to put in each sentence.

1. Charlie worked out the _____ between eighty-two and thirty-six.

2. The sum of forty and fifty has an _____ answer to a hundred minus ten.

3. Sue recorded her numbers in a _____ but John decided that his numbers looked better in a row.

4. The children entered the hall to _____ the instruments for their music lesson.

5. Multiplication is the _____ of division.

6. John and Sue discovered that the _____ of seven and nine was sixty-three.

▲ Connect each of the words in the top row to the word with a similar meaning in the bottom row. Looking up some of the words in a thesaurus might be helpful.

total	**decrease**	**changeless**	**repeat**	**enlarge**
recur	**increase**	**aggregate**	**constant**	**diminish**

▲ On the back of this sheet, write six separate sentences to show the meanings of each of these words.

factor	**quotient**	**calculator**	**mutliply**	**display**	**remainder**

© Hopscotch: *Literacy Trios* ▲ Mathematical vocabulary

Figure it out

▲ Find the answers to the clues and fill in the puzzles. Use the back of this sheet to do any working out.

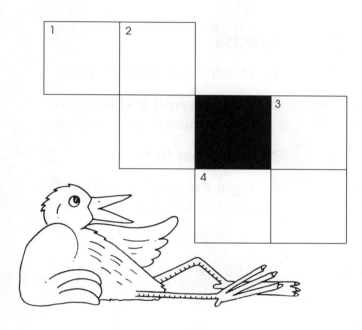

ACROSS

1. Thirteen add ten.

4. Forty-eight shared by two.

DOWN

2. Sixty-two minus thirty-one.

3. Seven times two.

▲ Think very carefully about what to do when solving these clues.

ACROSS

1. Add together twenty-three and fifty-three.

4. What is sixty-nine divided by three?

DOWN

2. Make thirty-one twice the size.

3. Subtract thirty-seven from fifty-nine.

Name _____

Figure it out

▲ Find the answers to the clues and fill in the puzzles. Use the back of this sheet to do any working out.

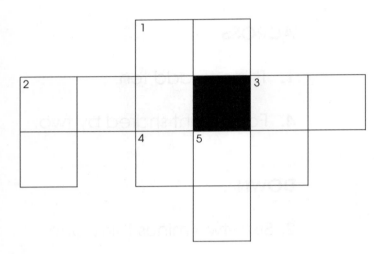

ACROSS

1. Eleven multiplied by five.

2. Five hundred and ten plus four hundred and sixty-nine.

3. Two times forty-one.

4. Eight hundred and fifty-two divided by four.

DOWN

1. 599 – 7   **2.** 31 x 3   **3.** 45 + 38   **5.** 689 – 677

ACROSS

1. 725 + 272   **3.** 968 – 227   **5.** 8 x 5   **7.** 48 ÷ 4

DOWN

2. Find the total of five hundred and forty-five and two hundred and thirty-four.

4. Find a half of two hundred and eighty-four.

6. How many threes in twenty-one?

© Hopscotch: *Literacy Trios* ▲ Mathematical vocabulary

Name _____

Figure it out

▲ Find the answers to the clues and fill in the puzzle. Do any working out on the back of this sheet.

ACROSS

1. Multiply five thousand, eight hundred and five by six.
5. Twenty divided into nine hundred and eighty.
6. Divide five thousand, three hundred and twenty-two into six equal groups. How many in each group?
7. Find a sixth of three thousand, one hundred and fifty.
9. What is the total of forty-seven and forty-six?
10. Add one thousand and eighty to the sum of nine hundred and forty plus five.
12. How many altogether is five hundred and nineteen, one hundred and seventeen and three hundred and thirty-seven?
13. Three hundred and eight divided by seven.
14. Share four thousand, three hundred and twenty by six, your answer by five, your answer by four, your answer by three.

DOWN

2. Sixty-four backwards.
3. Seven times larger than 4545.
4. 2262 plus 3254 add 1437.
8. The difference between ninety-four and thirty-nine.
9. The sum of 2127, 2527, 2085 and 2434.
10. Decrease sixty-five by thirty-nine.
11. A third of six hundred and seventy-two.

▲ Write in words the answers to the following clues.

5 across

_____

6 across

_____

10 across

_____

_____

3 down

_____

_____

Name _____

Missing words and letters

▲ Choose the right word or words from the list to put into each sentence.

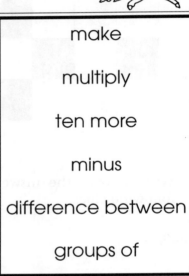

1. _____ _____ than twenty is thirty.

2. There are four _____ ____ three in twelve.

3. To _____ is to make something a number of times bigger.

4. The _____ _____ eleven and sixteen is five.

5. Nine and six _____ fifteen.

6. Nineteen _____ nine leaves ten.

make
multiply
ten more
minus
difference between
groups of

▲ Write out these words putting in the missing letters. Use a dictionary to help you.

tot __ l   altog __ th __ r   di __ isi __ n

_____   _____   _____

ad __ iti __ n   sub __ r __ ction   mult __ pli __ ation

_____   _____   _____

© Hopscotch: *Literacy Trios* ▲ Mathematical vocabulary

Missing words and letters

▲ Choose the most suitable word from the list to put into each sentence.

1. When you divide a number by two you _____ the number.

2. The answer to a multiplication problem is called the _____ .

3. Forty-four is twice as large as _____ – _____ .

4. The difference between twenty-two
   and forty-three is _____ – _____ .

5. When we _____ we make something
   a number of times larger.

6. A _____ is a number that will divide into
   another number with no remainder.

twenty-two

multiple

halve

multiply

product

twenty-one

▲ Work out the answers to each of these questions after first writing in the correct beginnings from the list below.

1. _____ 13 is subtracted from 40?

2. _____ 19 is 53?

3. _____ 27 and 68?

How many more than	What is the total of	How many are left when

▲ Write out these words on the back of this sheet putting in the missing letters. Use a dictionary to help you if you need to do so.

decr _ as _   inc _ ea _ e   alt _ ge _ her   quot _ e _ t

addi _ i _ n   subtr _ cti _ n   mul _ iplica _ ion   di _ isio _

Calculations

Missing words and letters

▲ Put the words on the signposts in the correct places in the sentences.

| multiplied | repeated | less | boundary | more | quotient |

1. The answer to a division calculation is called the _____ .

2. Multiplication is often referred to as _____ addition.

3. Fourteen _____ by five is seventy.

4. When adding thirty-three and twenty-nine you have to cross the tens _____ .

5. Fifty-three is _____ than fifty but _____ than sixty.

▲ Find the words that fit in place of the birds by choosing the letter of the most suitable answer below and writing it in the box at the end of each sentence.

1. To find the difference between two amounts I would do a 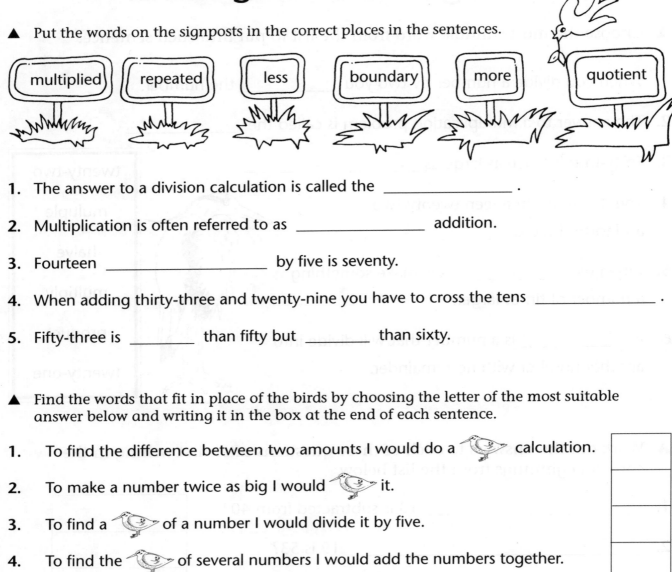 calculation.

2. To make a number twice as big I would ⬚ it.

3. To find a ⬚ of a number I would divide it by five.

4. To find the ⬚ of several numbers I would add the numbers together.

5. To make a number ⬚ the size I would share it by two.

| **A** total | **B** subtraction | **C** half | **D** fifth | **E** double |

▲ Some of the words in the two sentences below have letters missing. Rewrite the sentences correctly on the back of this sheet. Use a dictionary to help you.

1. The anwer to a multiplicaion sum is caled the produc.

2. The disply on the caculator gave Linda and Tom the answr they neded.

© Hopscotch: *Literacy Trios* ▲ Mathematical vocabulary

Name _____

Capital letters and punctuation

Remember that a sentence must begin with
a capital letter and end with a full stop

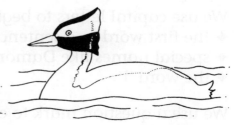

▲ Write out each of these sentences correctly.

1. the little boy held the coin in his hand

_____

2. the cost of the chocolate was seventy pence

_____

3. once Jenny had spent her money she went home

_____

4. the plate was not broken when Michael bought it

_____

5. the twins tried to sell their old toys at the jumble sale

_____

▲ Read this piece of writing. Circle the letters that should be in
capitals and put in the missing full stops.

the children spread their money on the counter in the shop they
were trying to work out how much they had there were four 1p
coins, three 5p coins and six 10p coins the shopkeeper helped
them by telling them they had 79p

Name _____

Capital letters and punctuation

We use capital letters to begin:
+ the first word in a sentence
+ special names like Damon or Glasgow
+ the word 'I'

We use a full stop:
+ at the end of a sentence
We might see a full stop:
+ after an abbreviation, e.g. Mr. or Mrs.

We use a question mark to end a sentence that asks a question.

▲ Write out each of these sentences correctly.

1. kara asked simon how much the bread cost

_____

2. when i was in france i bought some postcards

_____

3. mr and mrs collins sell toys in their shop

_____

4. a coin is a round and flat piece of metal used as money

_____

5. zoe said that she had spent all her money in london

_____

6. what is the price of this cake

_____

▲ Write this passage correctly on a separate piece of paper.
You will need to use capital letters, full stops, question marks, commas and speech marks.

lee bought an item costing £1 15 he paid for it using two one pound coins he tried to work out how much change he would receive the shop assistant said to lee that she thought he looked worried i am said lee because i cannot work out how much change i should get shall i help you work it out said the shop assistant

© Hopscotch: *Literacy Trios* ▲ Mathematical vocabulary

Capital letters and punctuation

We use capital letters to begin:
✦ the first word in a sentence.
✦ special names like Helen or Exeter.
✦ the word 'I'.

We use a full stop:
✦ at the end of a sentence.
We might see a full stop:
✦ after an abbreviation, e.g. Mr. or Mrs. or Dr.

We use a question mark to end a sentence that asks a question.
We use a comma to show a slight pause or break between parts of a sentence.
We use speech marks to identify words actually spoken.

▲ Write out each of these sentences correctly punctuated.

1. the calculation proved very difficult for the children to do

   _____

2. i cannot solve this puzzle said jean

   _____

3. what shall we do when we have worked out the best discount said Rebecca

   _____

4. mr and mrs tapping both agreed that it was too expensive to travel to cornwall by train

   _____

5. the supermarket sold many different types of product ranging from fruit bread and

   cooked meat to paint timber and garden furniture

   _____

   _____

▲ On the back of this sheet write a short passage to include the words shown below.
Also include at least 4 full stops, 1 question mark, 2 commas and 1 set of speech
marks. This is quite difficult but stay calm!

money   bought   pay   change   price   spent

Solving problems

Money wordsearch

▲ In the wordsearch are eight words to do with money.
Clues and some letters are given to help you. Search up,
down, back and across and write the words on the lines
when you find them. Some letters are used twice.

p	e	n	n	y	a	o	e
r	k	r	l	e	s	x	g
i	y	t	u	n	e	c	n
c	q	h	m	o	d	f	a
e	g	g	t	m	n	n	h
d	w	u	p	a	e	h	c
z	h	o	b	i	p	a	j
p	v	b	c	o	s	t	b

1. Small value coin. p _ _ _ y

_____

2. Money given back when
buying something. c h _ _ _ e

_____

3. Low in price. c _ _ _ p

_____

4. Use money to buy things. sp _ _ d _____

5. Cost of an item. p _ _ _ e _____

6. Coins and bank notes. m _ _ _ y _____

7. Amount you have to pay for something. c _ _ t _____

8. Gave money in exchange for goods. b _ _ g _ t _____

▲ Colour red all the letters you have used on the wordsearch.
Colour blue all the letters you have not used.

© Hopscotch: *Literacy Trios* ▲ Mathematical vocabulary

Name _____

Money wordsearch

▲ In this wordsearch are ten words all to do with buying and selling things. Find the words and write them down in the spaces provided. The first letter of each word is given as a clue. You will have to search in all directions except diagonally.

1. V _ _ _ _

2. E _ _ _ _ _ _ _ _

3. C _ _ _ _ _

4. P _ _ _ _

5. S _ _ _ _

6. B _ _ _ _ _

7. S _ _ _

8. A _ _ _ _ _

9. P _ _

10. P _ _ _ _

E	V	I	S	N	E	P	X	E
D	L	O	S	U	G	U	A	U
O	F	I	P	E	N	C	E	L
K	A	B	E	U	A	C	L	A
P	O	U	N	D	H	M	E	V
R	E	P	D	A	C	A	D	O
E	O	A	M	O	U	N	T	N
I	G	Y	U	H	I	E	J	I
B	O	U	G	H	T	P	O	Q

▲ Colour green all the letters you have used on the wordsearch. Colour yellow all the letters you have not used.

▲ Write down any other words you can find in the wordsearch. You may search for the words in all directions, including diagonally.

_____

_____

Name _____

Money wordsearch

▲ Hidden in this wordsearch are 14 words connected with money and the use of it. Clues and first letters are given to help you find each one. Write down each word when you find it and shade it in on the wordsearch. You will have to search in all directions.

S	P	E	N	D	E	U	Q	E	H	C	B
I	B	I	U	V	S	C	B	K	R	A	C
P	O	Q	A	G	O	A	I	T	N	P	A
C	C	L	H	S	J	P	C	K	S	I	E
A	U	F	T	Z	A	R	N	L	B	T	V
E	B	R	D	Y	E	O	Y	J	L	A	I
H	O	H	R	D	T	F	S	S	O	L	S
O	U	L	L	E	S	I	V	F	F	W	N
J	G	Z	P	T	N	T	E	X	G	M	E
D	H	T	N	U	O	C	S	I	D	L	P
I	T	N	Q	X	O	M	Y	N	Y	K	X
E	R	P	A	E	H	C	G	U	W	V	E

1. Piece of paper issued by a bank to serve as currency.   B

   _____

2. Wealth invested to produce more wealth.   C

   _____

3. Order to a bank to pay money.   C

   _____

4. Another name for money.   C

   _____

5. Made when expenditure exceeds income.   L

   _____

6. Made when income exceeds expenditure.   P _____

7. Very highly priced.   E _____

8. The amount of money something is worth.   V _____

9. Swapped money in exchange for goods.   B _____

10. Exchange something for money.   S _____

11. A 50p piece is one of these.   C _____

12. The amount that has to be paid.   C _____

13. Use money to buy things.   S _____

14. Low in price.   C _____

▲ Write down any other words you can find in the wordsearch.

_____

_____

_____

© Hopscotch: *Literacy Trios* ▲ Mathematical vocabulary

Name _____

Alphabetical mix-up

▲ Read the clues on the left.
Sort out the mixed-up letters in the middle.
Write the correct word in the box on the right.
The first letter of each word is written as a capital letter.

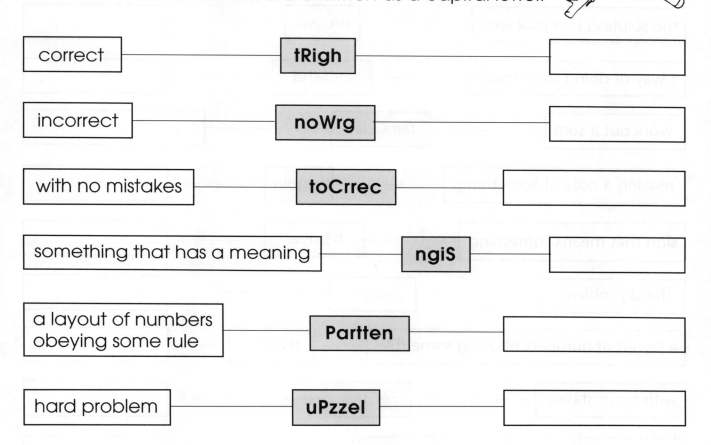

clue	mixed-up	answer
correct	**tRigh**	
incorrect	**noWrg**	
with no mistakes	**toCrrec**	
something that has a meaning	**ngiS**	
a layout of numbers obeying some rule	**Partten**	
hard problem	**uPzzel**	

▲ Sort out each set of mixed-up letters to make a money word.
The capital letter tells you which letter starts each word.

oiCn   **doPun**   **pSned**   **Cahnge**

_____   _____   _____   _____

▲ On the back of this sheet write four different sentences.
In each sentence use one of the words from the exercise above.

Name _____

Alphabetical mix-up

▲ Read the clues on the left. Sort out the mixed-up letters in
the middle. Write the correct word in the box on the right.
The first letter of each word is written as a capital letter.

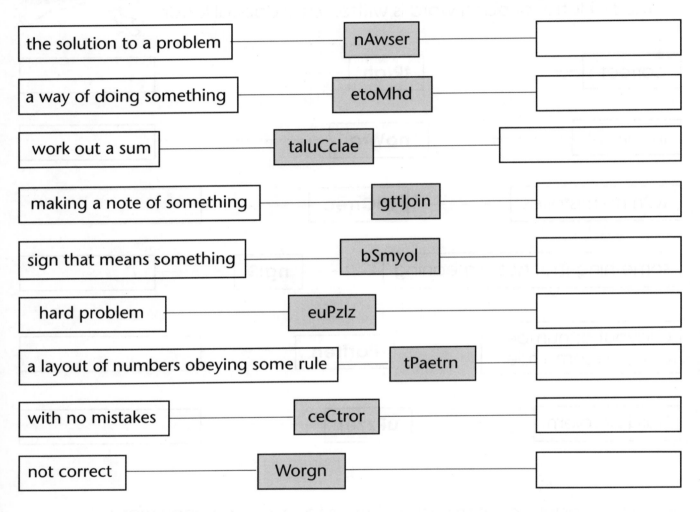

Clue	Mixed-up	Answer
the solution to a problem	nAwser	
a way of doing something	etoMhd	
work out a sum	taluCclae	
making a note of something	gttJoin	
sign that means something	bSmyol	
hard problem	euPzlz	
a layout of numbers obeying some rule	tPaetrn	
with no mistakes	ceCtror	
not correct	Worgn	

▲ Sort out each set of mixed-up letters to make a money word.
The capital letter tells you which letter starts each word.

tNoe   nPeyn   gBuoht   Epxsienve   aehCp

_____   _____   _____   _____   _____

▲ On the back of this sheet write five different sentences.
In each sentence include one of the words from the exercise above.

Solving problems

Alphabetical mix-up

▲ The sentences below have empty spaces where words should be.
The missing words are listed but their letters are all mixed up.
Rearrange the letters and write each word in the correct space.
To help you do this the first letter of each word has been written as a capital letter.

| nDtiucso | Ptorfi | aPttren | sLos | iuCltalcaon | lVaeu |

1. A _____ is a layout of numbers obeying some rule.

2. A mathematical problem solved in your head is called a mental _____ .

3. A business makes a _____ when its income exceeds its expenditure.

4. An amount of money taken off the full price of an item is called a _____ .

5. The monetary _____ of something is the amount of money that it is worth.

6. A business makes a _____ when its expenditure exceeds its income.

▲ Read the clues on the left. Sort out the mixed-up letters in the middle.
Write the correct word in the box on the right.
In order to help you the first letter of each word is written as a capital letter.

| sign that means something | loSmyb | |

| type of mathematical problem | ionEuaqt | |

| a way of doing something | thMedo | |

| very highly priced | exsEpeniv | |

| work out the answer to a sum | alCcaulte | |

▲ On the back of this sheet, write five different sentences. In each sentence
include a different word from the boxes on the right in the exercise above.

© Hopscotch: *Literacy Trios* ▲ Mathematical vocabulary

Name _____

Time teasers

▲ Write these sentences in a more sensible order.

1. At the zoo on Tuesday the monkeys pulled faces at my Dad.
2. The following day we came home.
3. On Monday it rained all day and Fiona fell in a puddle.
4. Wednesday and Thursday were really hot so we went on the beach.
5. Last week we went on holiday.
6. Mum got sunburnt and her face went the colour of a beetroot.
7. We left home on Sunday at eight o'clock in the morning.
8. On Friday my sister was ill so we could not do much.

1. _____

2. _____

3. _____

4. _____

5. _____

6. _____

7. _____

8. _____

▲ On the back of this sheet write out these jumbled months in order starting with January.

May   November   April   September   February   July

June   March   December   August   January   October

    © Hopscotch: *Literacy Trios* ▲ Mathematical vocabulary

Name _____

Time teasers

▲ Arrange these words in order starting with the word that indicates the longest time span.

morning	second	day	weekend	month	leap year
minute	millennium	hour	fortnight	century	year	week

_____

_____

▲ Make up four sentences each of which includes two different words chosen from the list. You must use a word from the list only once.

always	never	birthday	holiday	noon	midnight
yesterday	tomorrow	before	after	afternoon	evening

1. _____

2. _____

3. _____

4. _____

▲ Make these sentences make sense by joining the right parts with a line.

Your date of birth is	times at which certain things will happen.
A timetable is a list of	is winter.
A calendar is a list of	the day, month and year when you were born.
The season after autumn	days, weeks and months of the year.

Name _____

Time teasers

▲ Read the clues on the left, sort out the words in the middle and write each word in the most appropriate place in the column on the right.

Clue	Word	Correct order
the day after today	yesterday	
a list of days, weeks, months	never	
a period of 2 weeks	calendar	
this day	century	
a period of 1000 years	fortnight	
Saturday and Sunday	always	
the day before today	tomorrow	
a period of 100 years	millennium	
at all times	today	
not ever, at no time	weekend	

▲ The words in capital letters are in the wrong places. Sort them out and write the most suitable word opposite the correct sentence number in the box provided.

1. There are sixty HOURS in one minute and sixty SECONDS in one hour.

2. An HALF clock face shows the time using traditional hands.

3. A DIGITAL consists of twenty-four QUARTER.

4. MINUTES to nine is the same as eight forty-five.

5. A DISPLAY watch shows the time as a DAY of numbers.

6. ANALOGUE past six is the same time as six thirty.

1.
2.
3.
4.
5.
6.

▲ On the back of this sheet, do a short piece of writing that includes all of these words.

Monday   holiday   fast   February

birthday   evening   arrive

© Hopscotch: *Literacy Trios* ▲ Mathematical vocabulary

Name _____

Joining sentences

▲ Join the two sentences together using the best word from the list. Try to use each word only once.

1. The ball was round. The brick was square.

   _____

2. I rushed home. I had to make a telephone call.

   _____

3. A sphere will roll. It has a curved surface.

   _____

4. The needle was sharp. I left it where it was.

   _____

5. A cube has six flat surfaces. It has twelve edges.

   _____

so	because	as	but	and

Finish both these sentences in your own words.

1. I carried on drawing until _____

   _____

2. Chris built his model car when _____

   _____

Name _____

Joining sentences

By using joining words we can often make two sentences into one.
Examples of joining words are: and, but, as, so, because, until, when.

▲ Join the two sentences together using the most suitable word from those given above. Try to use a different joining word for each set of sentences.

1. It was a slippery surface. We had to tread carefully.

_____

2. Jenny looked at the diagram. She could not remember how to fit the

model together. _____

_____

3. The cube was solid. It weighed very little.

_____

4. I was walking round the corner this morning. I saw the accident.

_____

5. It was a 3D shape with a round base and a pointed top. I knew that it must

be a cone. _____

_____

6. I cannot come to tea. I have drawn these triangles.

_____

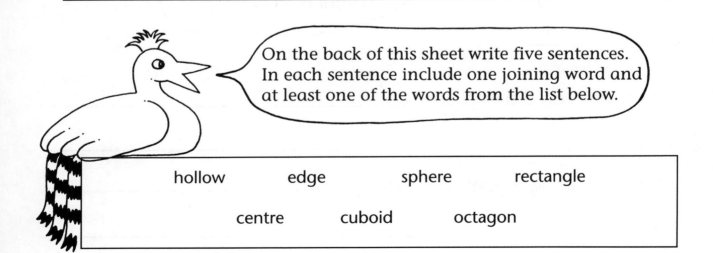

On the back of this sheet write five sentences. In each sentence include one joining word and at least one of the words from the list below.

| hollow | edge | sphere | rectangle |
| centre | cuboid | octagon | |

© Hopscotch: *Literacy Trios* ▲ Mathematical vocabulary

Measures, shape and space

Joining sentences

By using connecting words we can often make two or more sentences into one. Examples of connecting words are: and, but, as, so, because, until, when, therefore, however.

▲ Connect these sets of sentences together choosing the most appropriate word from those given above. Try to use as many different connecting words as you can. Some of the sentences will need to be rearranged before you join them together.

1. The side of a sphere is curved. A sphere will roll.

   _____

2. It was heavy. The child had difficulty lifting the solid object. It was bulky.

   _____

3. Both go to a point at the top. A pyramid usually has a square base. A cone has a

   round base. _____

   _____

4. Her results were sometimes disappointing. Pam enjoyed drawing shapes of many kinds.

   She did not work neatly. _____

   _____

5. It helped him with his technology work at school. John liked to use his construction kit.

   _____

6. I was standing at the intersection of the two roads. It ran down the disused railway line.

   I saw the escaped tiger. _____

   _____

On the back of this sheet write six sentences. In each sentence include two joining words and at least one of the words from the list below.

convex	straight	surface	cylinder
rectangular	hexagon	build	concave

Measures, shape and space

What is it?

▲ Name the 2-D (flat) shape hidden in each of these clues. Choose your answers from the list at the bottom of the page.

1. round   **2.** five sides   **3.** six sides

4. three sides   **5.** four sides   **6.** four even sides

1.	**2.**	**3.**
4.	**5.**	**6.**

▲ Name the 3-D (solid) shape hidden in each of these clues. Choose your answers from the box at the bottom of the page.

1. six square faces   **2.** shaped like a ball

3. tube-shaped   **4.** round base and a pointed top

1.	**2.**
3.	**4.**

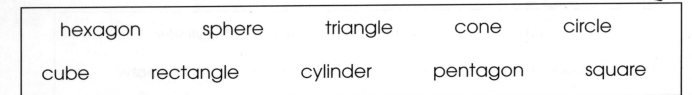

▲ On the back of this sheet draw and name the ten shapes given in the box below. Draw carefully and use a ruler for any straight edges. Colour in the shapes.

hexagon	sphere	triangle	cone	circle
cube	rectangle	cylinder	pentagon	square

Name _____

What is it?

▲ Name the shape hidden in each of these clues. Choose your answers from the list below the questions.

1. 3-D with 6 square faces.
2. Round and 2-D.
3. 2-D with 6 sides.
4. 2-D with 4 sides and 4 right angles.
5. 3-D with the same shape along all its length.
6. Round and 3-D.
7. 2-D with 5 sides.
8. 3-D tube-shaped object.

9. 2-D with 4 equal sides and 4 right angles.
10. Any 2-D shape with edges that are straight.
11. 3-D with 6 faces that are rectangles (not squares).
12. 2-D with 8 sides.
13. 3-D with a round base and a pointed top.
14. 2-D with 3 sides.

| square | cuboid | cone | hexagon | prism | octagon | rectangle |
| pentagon | sphere | circle | triangle | polygon | cylinder | cube |

1.	2.	3.	4.
5.	6.	7.	8.
9.	10.	11.	12
		13.	14.

▲ Answer these questions on a separate piece paper. What does it mean if something is:

spherical?   cylindrical?   three-dimensional?

On the back of this sheet draw and name ten of the shapes you have identified from the clues. Draw carefully and then colour in the shapes.

Name _____

What is it?

▲ Name the shape hidden in each of these clues. Choose your answers from the list below the questions. Use a mathematical dictionary to help you.

1. 2-D with 3 sides.

2. 2-D with 8 sides.

3. Half a circle.

4. 3-D with 6 square faces.

5. Any 3-D shape with a number of faces.

6. Parallelogram with all 4 sides equal.

7. 3-D with a round base and a pointed top.

8. 2-D with 5 sides.

9. 3-D with 8 faces.

10. Round and 2-D.

11. 3-D tube-shaped object.

12. 2-D with 6 sides.

13. 3-D polygon base with triangular sides rising up to a point.

14. 2-D with 4 sides and 4 right angles.

15. 2-D with 4 equal sides and 4 right angles.

16. 3-D with 6 faces that are rectangles (not squares).

17. Any 2-D shape with edges that are straight.

18. Round and 3-D.

19. 3-D with 4 triangular faces.

20. Half a sphere.

polyhedron	square	cuboid	pyramid cone	hexagon	octagon	hemisphere
rectangle	pentagon	sphere	circle	triangle	polygon
octahedron	semicircle	tetrahedron	rhombus	cylinder	cube

1.	2.	3.	4.
5.	6.	7.	8.
9.	10.	11.	12.
13.	14.	15.	16.
17.	18.	19.	20.

▲ Answer these questions in complete sentences on the back of this sheet. What is:

an equilateral triangle?   an isosceles triangle?   a scalene triangle?

© Hopscotch: *Literacy Trios* ▲ Mathematical vocabulary

Measures, shape and space

Name _____

Find the antonym

▲ Look for ten words in the wordsearch that have the opposite meaning to the words in the list. Circle and connect the words together as shown.

To help you, the start letter of each word in the wordsearch has been written as a capital letter and shaded.

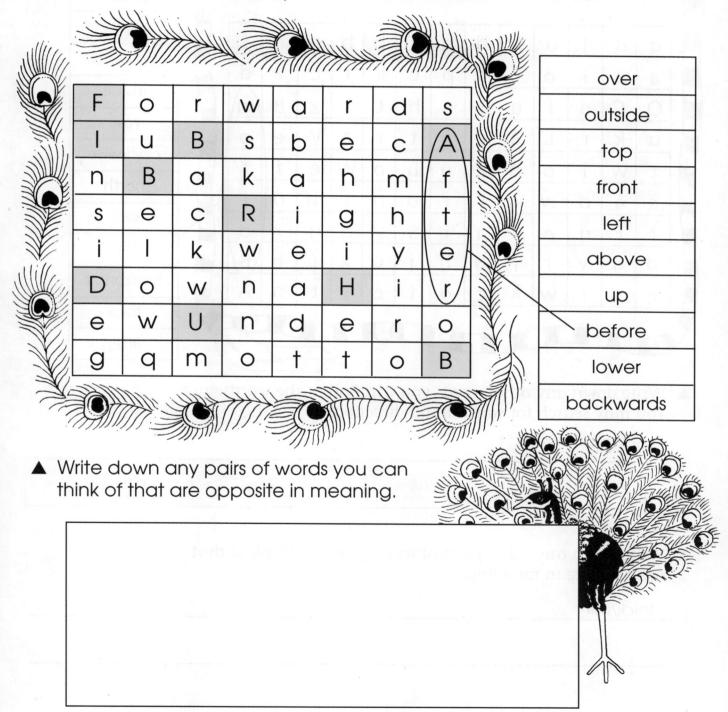

F	o	r	w	a	r	d	s
l	u	B	s	b	e	c	A
n	B	a	k	a	h	m	f
s	e	c	R	i	g	h	t
i	l	k	w	e	i	y	e
D	o	w	n	a	H	i	r
e	w	U	n	d	e	r	o
g	q	m	o	t	t	o	B

| over |
| outside |
| top |
| front |
| left |
| above |
| up |
| before |
| lower |
| backwards |

▲ Write down any pairs of words you can think of that are opposite in meaning.

Name _____

Find the antonym

▲ Look for 12 words in the wordsearch which have the opposite meaning
to the words in the list. Circle and connect the words together as shown.
Search in all directions except diagonally. To help you, the start letter of
each word in the wordsearch is written as a capital letter.

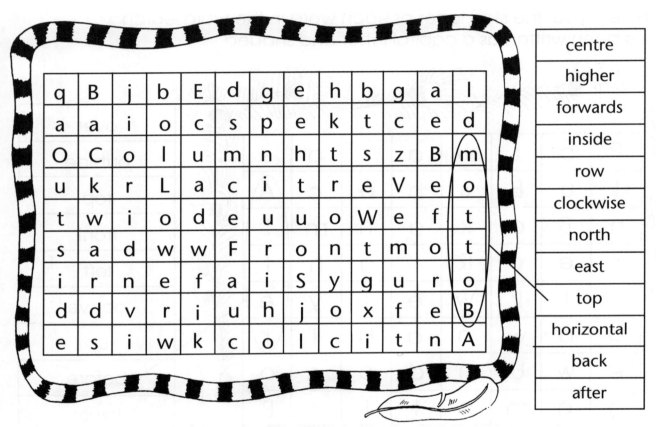

q	B	j	b	E	d	g	e	h	b	g	a	l
a	a	i	o	c	s	p	e	k	t	c	e	d
O	C	o	l	u	m	n	h	t	s	z	B	m
u	k	r	L	a	c	i	t	r	e	V	e	o
t	w	i	o	d	e	u	u	o	W	e	f	t
s	a	d	w	w	F	r	o	n	t	m	o	t
i	r	n	e	f	a	i	S	y	g	u	r	o
d	d	v	r	j	u	h	j	o	x	f	e	B
e	s	i	w	k	c	o	l	c	i	t	n	A

| centre |
| higher |
| forwards |
| inside |
| row |
| clockwise |
| north |
| east |
| top |
| horizontal |
| back |
| after |

▲ Write down any other words you can find in the wordsearch.
You may search for words in all directions.

_____

_____

▲ Write down any other pairs of words you can think of that
are opposite in meaning.

thick/thin _____

_____

© Hopscotch: *Literacy Trios* ▲ Mathematical vocabulary

Measures, shape and space

Find the antonym

An antonym is a word with a meaning opposite to another.
A word can have more than one antonym.

▲ Find the 20 words in the wordsearch which have the opposite meaning to the words in the list. Circle and connect the words together as shown. Search in all directions.

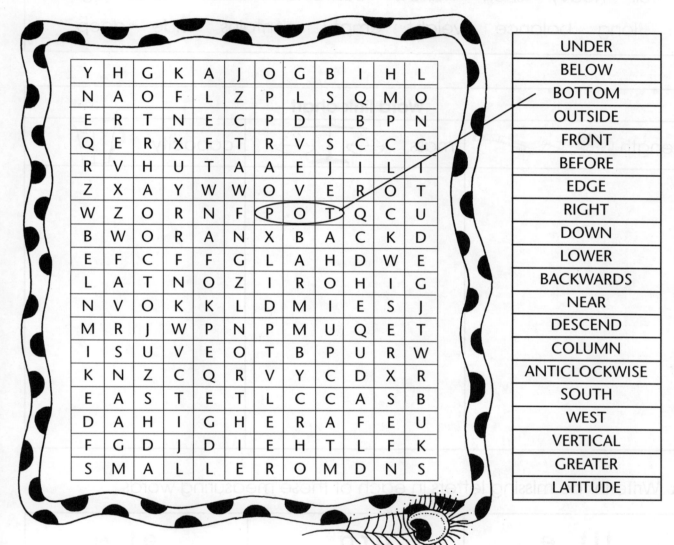

Y	H	G	K	A	J	O	G	B	I	H	L
N	A	O	F	L	Z	P	L	S	Q	M	O
E	R	T	N	E	C	P	D	I	B	P	N
Q	E	R	X	F	T	R	V	S	C	C	G
R	V	H	U	T	A	A	E	J	I	L	I
Z	X	A	Y	W	W	O	V	E	R	O	T
W	Z	O	R	N	F	P	O	T	Q	C	U
B	W	O	R	A	N	X	B	A	C	K	D
E	F	C	F	F	G	L	A	H	D	W	E
L	A	T	N	O	Z	I	R	O	H	I	G
N	V	O	K	K	L	D	M	I	E	S	J
M	R	J	W	P	N	P	M	U	Q	E	T
I	S	U	V	E	O	T	B	P	U	R	W
K	N	Z	C	Q	R	V	Y	C	D	X	R
E	A	S	T	E	T	L	C	C	A	S	B
D	A	H	I	G	H	E	R	A	F	E	U
F	G	D	J	D	I	E	H	T	L	F	K
S	M	A	L	L	E	R	O	M	D	N	S

UNDER
BELOW
BOTTOM
OUTSIDE
FRONT
BEFORE
EDGE
RIGHT
DOWN
LOWER
BACKWARDS
NEAR
DESCEND
COLUMN
ANTICLOCKWISE
SOUTH
WEST
VERTICAL
GREATER
LATITUDE

▲ Select other words of your own and write two antonyms to go with each.
One has been done for you.

 accept – reject, refuse _____

_____

_____

_____

Measuring words

▲ Read these words and write each one in the correct box.

full   heavy   short   narrow   container   scales   holds   light
long   balance   weight   empty   contains   wide   deep

Word link chart		
length	mass	capacity

▲ Write in the missing letters in each of these measuring words.

lit_e	gra_	_etre
cent_m_tre	milli_it_e	k_log_am

▲ Write this sentence in the correct order on the back of this sheet.

(100 centimetres.)   (A metre is)   (the same length as)

    © Hopscotch: *Literacy Trios* ▲ Mathematical vocabulary

Name _____

Measuring words

▲ Complete these sentences using only the words shown in the box.
The words can be used more than once.

1. A centimetre is longer than a _____ .

2. A _____ is the longest measurement
shown in the word box.

3. A _____ is the shortest
measurement recorded in the word box.

4. A metre is shorter than both a _____
and a _____ .

5. A metre is longer than a _____ or a
_____ but not as long as a
_____ or a _____ .

mile
metre
kilometre
millimetre
centimetre

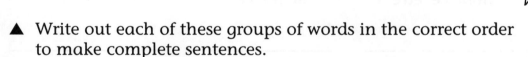

▲ Write out each of these groups of words in the correct order
to make complete sentences.

1. (of a surface) (The size) (is called the area.)

_____

2. (measuring how) (Scales are an) (much things weigh.)
(instrument for) _____

_____

3. (The capacity of) (will hold.) (is how much it) (a container)

_____

Measures, shape and space

Measuring words

▲ Complete each of these sentences with a suitable beginning or ending.
Use a dictionary or other reference material to help you.

1. The *perimeter* is _____

2. _____ is called the *circumference*.

3. *Capacity* is the _____

4. _____ is called the *area*.

5. The *surface* is the _____

6. The *breadth* of something is _____

▲ Arrange each group of letters to spell a measuring word.

ga on ll	log ram ki	nce di sta	ty e mp
_____	_____	_____	_____
ba ce lan	ntim ce etre	ili tre cent	ki re lomet
_____	_____	_____	_____
lil mil itre	vie st hea	sh low al	un ce o
_____	_____	_____	_____

▲ On the back of this sheet write out each of these jumbled sentences so that they make complete sense. Have patience – this is not an easy exercise!

1. amount is is almost An approximate not completely so. one that exact but

2. thousandth of is equivalent a metre. A millimetre to one

3. imperial measurements Miles, yards, feet of length. are all and inches

4. of mass. Tonnes, kilograms metric measurements and grams are all

© Hopscotch: *Literacy Trios* ▲ Mathematical vocabulary

Name _____

Definitions

Use a dictionary to help you with the words on this page.

▲ Join each word to its meaning. One has been done for you.

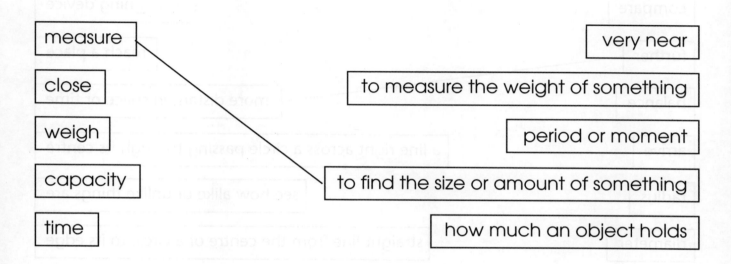

measure	very near
close	to measure the weight of something
weigh	period or moment
capacity	to find the size or amount of something
time	how much an object holds

▲ Complete each word or write the meaning in the empty box.

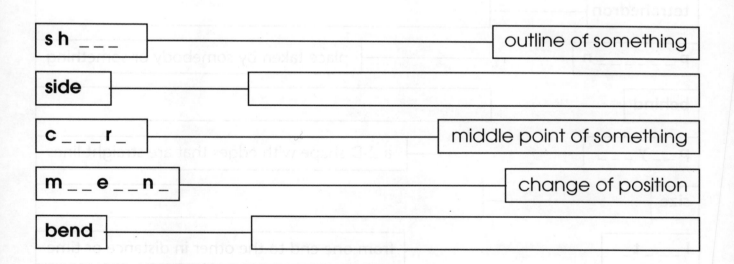

s h _ _ _	outline of something
side	
c _ _ _ r _	middle point of something
m _ _ e _ _ n _	change of position
bend	

▲ On the back of this sheet, write down these words with their meanings.

size	width
minute	
twice	hollow

Name _____

Definitions

Use a dictionary to help you with the words on this page.

▲ Join each word to its meaning. One has been done for you.

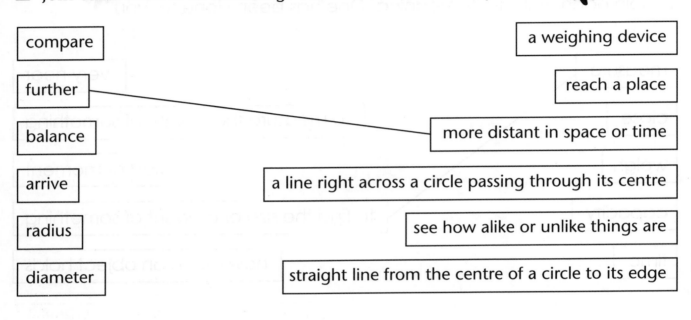

compare		a weighing device
further		reach a place
balance		more distant in space or time
arrive		a line right across a circle passing through its centre
radius		see how alike or unlike things are
diameter		straight line from the centre of a circle to its edge

▲ Complete each word or write the meaning in the empty box.

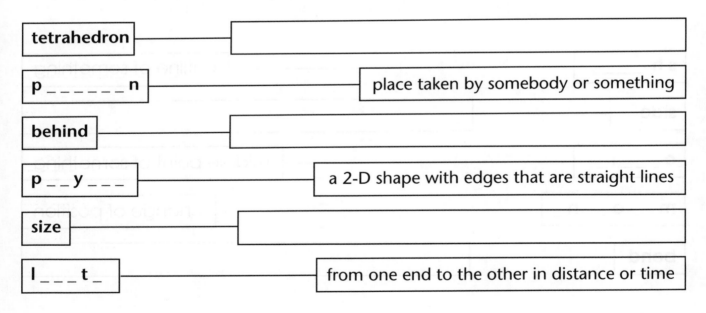

tetrahedron	
p _ _ _ _ _ n	place taken by somebody or something
behind	
p _ _ y _ _ _	a 2-D shape with edges that are straight lines
size	
l _ _ _ t _	from one end to the other in distance or time

▲ On the back of this sheet, write down these words with their meanings.

stretch   diagonal   route   underneath   symmetrical   heptagon

© Hopscotch: *Literacy Trios* ▲ Mathematical vocabulary

Name _____

Definitions

Use a dictionary to help you with the words on this page.

▲ Join each word to its definition. One has been done for you.

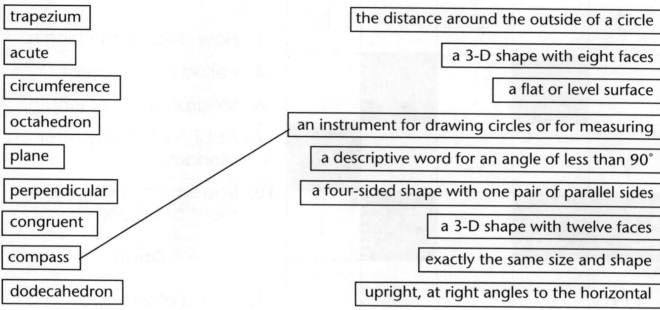

trapezium	the distance around the outside of a circle
acute	a 3-D shape with eight faces
circumference	a flat or level surface
octahedron	an instrument for drawing circles or for measuring
plane	a descriptive word for an angle of less than 90°
perpendicular	a four-sided shape with one pair of parallel sides
congruent	a 3-D shape with twelve faces
compass	exactly the same size and shape
dodecahedron	upright, at right angles to the horizontal

▲ Write down a word to fit the meaning or a meaning to fit the word.

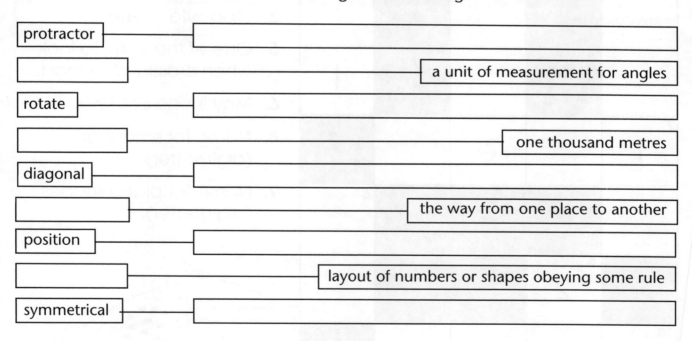

protractor

a unit of measurement for angles

rotate

one thousand metres

diagonal

the way from one place to another

position

layout of numbers or shapes obeying some rule

symmetrical

▲ On the back of this sheet, write down these words with their meanings.

parallelogram   prism   vertex   angle   concentric   compare   quadrilateral

Solve it

▲ Work out the clues and fill in the crossword grid.

¹d		²p		³h
⁴y		a		
				⁵l
⁶m		t		
				t
⁷T		e		
				⁸
	⁹2			
¹⁰e		g		

Across

1. How deep something is.
4. Period of 12 months.
6. Measurement of length.
7. Abbr. for the day after Monday.
10. Line where two surfaces meet at an angle.

Down

1. Period of 24 hours.
2. Break between lessons.
3. Opposite of **she**.
5. One of the ways to look when crossing the road.
6. May is one of these.
8. Name for solid shapes (digit/letter).
9. Name for plane shapes (digit/letter).

© Hopscotch: *Literacy Trios* ▲ Mathematical vocabulary

Name _____

Solve it

▲ Work out the clues and fill in the crossword.

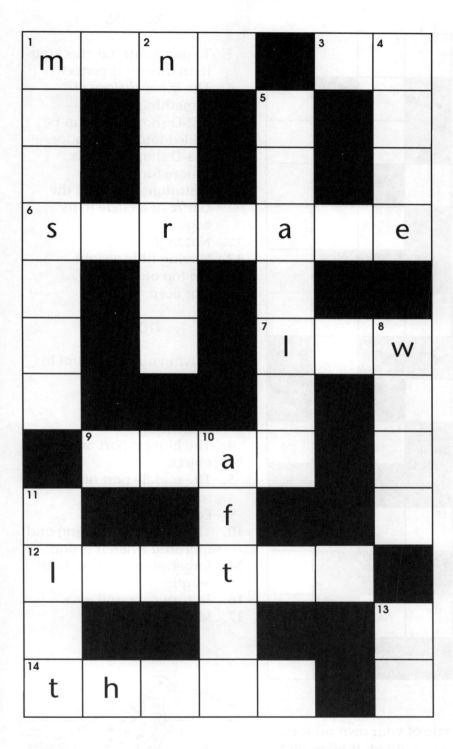

ACROSS

1. Great in number.
3. Before noon.
6. The outside covering of something.
7. Not high.
9. Make a picture by putting marks on a surface.
12. Small or tiny.
14. Number 3 is the
 _ _ _ _ _ number.

DOWN

1. Find the size or amount of something.
2. Almost.
4. A greater amount or number.
5. Not deep.
8. Great in breadth.
10. Later in time.
11. Level and smooth.
13. After noon.

▲ Try and make up a crossword puzzle of your own.
Give it to one of your friends to do. You will need squared
paper, a ruler, a pencil and a dictionary. Good luck!

Name _____

Solve it

▲ Work out the clues and complete the crossword.

ACROSS

1. To guess without checking if an answer is correct.
6. The inner surface of something.
7. A 2-D shape that can be folded into a 3-D shape.
8. A 3-D shape with six square faces.
11. A straight line from the centre of a circle to its edge.
12. Not high.
13. Having little weight.
15. On top of.
18. Not deep.

DOWN

1. Having all sides equal in length.
2. A day of the week.
3. The centre point of something.
4. The highest part of an object.
5. The middle part of something.
9. Earlier in time.
10. Time between evening and morning when it is dark.
14. Imperial measurement of length.
16. To turn over and over.
17. Made long ago.

▲ Try making up a crossword puzzle of your own on some squared paper. You will have to be patient. It takes quite a while to make all the words fit together. Start with a 10 x 10 grid and fit the words into it. Do not number the squares or write the clues until you have got all your words fitted together. When finished ask a friend to do the puzzle.

© Hopscotch: *Literacy Trios* ▲ Mathematical vocabulary

Making sentences

▲ Put the groups of words below into sentences in two ways.
Remember to use capital letters and full stops correctly.
The first group has been done for you.

1. when I got home, it was 6 o'clock, to my surprise

To my surprise it was 6 o'clock when I got home.

When I got home to my surprise it was 6 o'clock.

2. John and Cathy, in the afternoon, painted, some shapes

_____

_____

3. at the end of, a container, the pier, was floating in the sea

_____

_____

▲ On another sheet of paper, do the same with these word groups.

1. spent, the money, quickly, the people

2. was carefully, outside the house, a car, parked

3. morning, as usual, yesterday, I went to school

4. walked, every day, to the park, the children, happily

5. the pencil, measured the length of, carefully, the children

Name _____

Making sentences

▲ Put the groups of words below into sentences in two ways.
Remember to use capital letters and full stops correctly.
The first group has been done for you.

1. went to the swimming baths, in the morning, Scott and his friends

   Scott and his friends went to the swimming baths in the morning.

   In the morning Scott and his friends went to the swimming baths.

2. not raining, I go for many walks, in summer, when it is

   _____

   _____

3. in winter, to the hillside, as the snow is falling, we take our sledges

   _____

   _____

4. gazed down on to, the people, the lake, for a minute or two

   _____

   _____

▲ On another sheet of paper, do the same with these word groups.

1. quickly, appeared, round the corner, the cat

2. and went inside, I left, slowly, the garden

3. up and down, shouting for help, the man ran, the pavement

4. stood out, above the carpet of mist, clearly, the top of the pyramid

5. lifted the, glass prism, the girl, carefully

6. agreed to, with whole-hearted approval, the children, do better

© Hopscotch: *Literacy Trios* ▲ Mathematical vocabulary

Making sentences

▲ Make up six sentences by selecting groups of words from the chart.
Include one set of words from a shaded box in each sentence.

was carefully	the pier	parked	when it is
the lake	a container	every day	for a minute or two
happily	not raining	clearly	to my surprise
I left	the children	at the end of	walked
when I got home	to the park	slowly	above the carpet of mist
stood out	do better	I go for many walks	outside the house
gazed down on to	a car	the people	with whole-hearted approval
agreed to	and went inside	it was six o'clock	the top of the pyramid
was floating in the sea	in summer	the garden	the children

1. _____

2. _____

3. _____

4. _____

5. _____

6. _____

▲ Now do the same with the sets of words on this chart. You will need another sheet of paper.

morning	the cat	the children	went to the swimming baths
we take our sledges	spent	to the hillside	shouting for help
John and Cathy	in the morning	lifted the	yesterday
up and down	Scott	the money	round the corner
carefully	as usual	the man ran	as the snow is falling
glass prism	the pavement	in the afternoon	the girl
quickly	painted	the pencil	I went to school
and his friends	quickly	appeared	measured the length of
in winter	the people	some shapes	carefully

True or false?

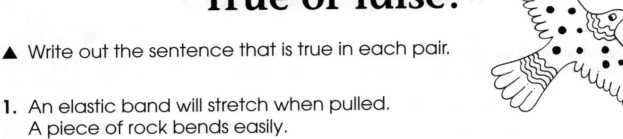

▲ Write out the sentence that is true in each pair.

1. An elastic band will stretch when pulled.
   A piece of rock bends easily.

   _____

2. The middle of a circle is at the edge.
   The large hand on a clock does a whole turn every hour.

   _____

3. A pentagon has six sides.
   An octagon has eight sides.

   _____

4. A cube is a 2-D shape with six faces and twelve edges.
   A pyramid has sides in the shape of a triangle.

   _____

▲ On another sheet of paper, write out the sentence
  that is false in each pair.

1. A point is very much like a straight line.
   To sort is to put things into sets or groups.

2. The day before Wednesday is Thursday.
   Sunday is the day after Saturday.

3. Height is the length from the bottom to the top of something.
   Width is the distance from London to Glasgow.

4. A centimetre is shorter than a metre.
   A metre stick has a length of ten centimetres.

© Hopscotch: *Literacy Trios* ▲ Mathematical vocabulary

Name _____

True or false?

▲ Write out the sentence that is true in each pair.

1. Compasses are an ideal instrument for finding direction.
   A reading of 90° with an angle measurer indicates a right angle.

   _____

2. An angle of 75° is smaller than an angle of 90°.
   On the points of a compass NE is opposite to SE.

   _____

3. The picture you see in a mirror or calm water is called a reflection.
   The sides of an equilateral triangle are of different lengths.

   _____

4. An isosceles triangle has five sides.
   A line of symmetry is a line that divides a shape exactly in half.

   _____

5. A polyhedron is a 2-D shape with any number of faces.
   Curved faces can be found on a sphere, a cone and a cylinder.

   _____

▲ Write your answers to this section on a separate piece of paper.
Each of the following sentences is untrue. Can you say why?
Begin your answer like this: *Sentence 1 is untrue because…*

1. A regular shape is one in which all the sides are of unequal length.

2. Centimetres, grams and litres are all imperial measurements.

3. Examples of metric measures are miles, inches and pints.

4. The ten months of the year are grouped into three seasons.

5. There are one hundred millilitres in one litre.

Name _____

True or false?

▲ Write out the sentence that is true in each pair.

1. A kite is a quadrilateral with two pairs of equal sides which are not opposite to each other.
Intersecting lines are lines that are the same distance apart along their full length.

_____

2. A millennium is a period of one thousand years.
A millilitre is equivalent to one thousand litres.

_____

3. The circumference of a circle is the distance from its centre to its edge.
The distance around the outside of an area is called the perimeter.

_____

▲ Each of the following sentences is untrue. Can you say why?
Begin your answer like this: *Sentence 1 is untrue because…*

1. A reflex angle is an angle that is more than 90° and less than 360°.

_____

2. An angle of less than 90° is called an obtuse angle.

_____

3. There are five right angles in a complete turn.

_____

4. An irregular shape is one in which all the sides are of equal length.

_____

▲ Continue treating each sentence in the same way as in Section 2
above but write down the answers on a separate piece of paper.

1. A cuboid is a four-sided shape with opposite sides equal
and parallel.

2. A convex surface curves inwards like an upturned saucer.

© Hopscotch: *Literacy Trios* ▲ Mathematical vocabulary

Name _____

Squares

This is a word building game.
You must go to a square that is touching the letter you are on.
That square can be above, below, to the side or in the corner.

▲ Use the letter grid to build the ten words in the list. Shade in the letters as you build the word. One has been done for you.

a	t	w	f	a	b	e	c	c
a	s	a	e	r	o	r	n	o
l	t	h	g	i	u	n	d	r
l	s	e	d	d	s	a	p	m
e	g	t	i	l	r	s	c	o
s	i	z	t	e	y	l	s	f
s	l	e	h	g	i	n	r	o
s	r	o	o	r	t	a	r	k
t	a	f	w	i	e	j	c	a

weighs
across
star
compare
fortnight
size
tall
around
slide
corner

▲ Can you find any more words on the grid in the same way?
If you can then write the words on the lines below.

_____

_____

Name _____

Squares

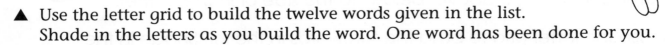

This is a word building game.
You must go to a square that is touching the letter you are on.
That square can be above, below, to the side or in the corner.

▲ Use the letter grid to build the twelve words given in the list.
Shade in the letters as you build the word. One word has been done for you.

T	S	B	R	M	R	L	I	L	Q	N
U	O	O	L	R	I	V	L	I	A	R
G	U	S	T	O	A	E	T	W	O	R
H	O	P	G	N	I	R	R	C	N	S
K	L	T	H	G	E	N	O	U	D	I
M	I	Y	X	E	V	N	N	I	L	A
L	O	G	S	R	R	D	G	L	A	T
M	A	R	K	I	E	E	R	I	T	N
J	I	S	H	D	Z	A	T	H	O	E
U	C	F	E	A	L	E	E	C	G	D
E	R	V	D	U	P	C	M	R	E	G
I	R	R	E	G	A	E	I	B	E	P

ROUGHLY
NARROW
PERIMETER
KILOGRAM
CONTAINS
MILLILITRE
DIGITAL
SHAPE
STRAIGHT
CURVED
IRREGULAR
CONVEX

▲ Can you find any more words on the grid in the same way?
If you can then write the words on the lines below.

_____

_____

© Hopscotch: *Literacy Trios* ▲ Mathematical vocabulary

Name _____

Squares

This is a word building activity.
You have to build words by going from one square to another.
You must go to a square that is touching the letter you are on.
That square can be above, below, to the side or in the corner.

▲ Use the letter grid to build the twenty words given in the list.
Shade in the letters as you build the word. You can use some letters more than once.
One word has been done for you.

A	C	Y	S	T	R	I	A	Z	I	M	D	B	S	B
P	P	O	F	I	C	E	N	T	C	E	W	L	I	X
O	B	U	Z	A	T	F	N	G	R	T	I	R	Y	E
X	U	R	T	H	A	E	U	L	E	D	R	T	H	D
N	D	E	W	E	V	A	R	A	E	E	U	U	T	A
A	R	B	S	C	R	L	V	E	L	F	B	N	Y	P
N	R	T	P	A	S	L	E	C	T	I	O	O	R	S
C	E	A	T	H	Y	G	L	Q	Y	D	R	T	P	I
S	O	O	F	M	M	E	S	R	Q	A	H	T	O	R
E	M	O	C	A	G	O	T	U	N	S	C	D	O	S
A	T	K	R	T	N	T	A	L	Y	J	E	M	I	H
A	T	D	L	A	K	D	L	A	G	A	W	T	P	E
N	I	C	N	J	R	I	E	R	I	N	A	G	H	D
L	H	A	S	W	L	A	T	C	L	O	N	O	I	G
F	R	R	O	K	S	U	R	Y	L	A	C	A	O	N
E	M	Y	E	E	A	R	E	L	A	C	I	R	G	R
O	U	E	M	T	N	E	M	Q	I	I	P	U	C	A
J	R	N	H	C	T	D	C	N	D	R	L	A	R	M

BIRTHDAY
OPPOSITE
FURTHEST
CENTIMETRE
UNDERNEATH
REFLECTION
PARALLEL
JOURNEY
MEASUREMENT
COORDINATES
SYMMETRY
NARROW
OCTAGONAL
PROTRACTOR
QUADRILATERAL
TRIANGULAR
CYLINDRICAL
SIDEWAYS
HEPTAGON
DIAGRAM

▲ Now draw the word grid again on squared paper. See how many words
you can build that are not shown in the above list. Try and build as many
words as you can. Each word must have at least five letters.

© Hopscotch: *Literacy Trios* ▲ Mathematical vocabulary

Name _____

Word games

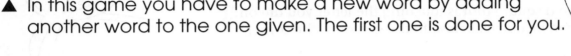

▲ In this game you have to make a new word by adding another word to the one given. The first one is done for you.

1. Make **end** to mean *Saturday and Sunday*. | w e e k e n d

2. Make **time** to mean *going to bed*. | b _ _ t i m e

3. Make **cross** to mean *from one side to the other*. | _ c r o s s

4. Make **ways** to mean *walking like a crab*. | s _ _ _ w a y s

5. Make **side** to mean *next to*. | b _ s i d e

6. Make **times** to mean *every now and again*. | s _ _ _ t i m e s

▲ Now make a new word by adding letters to the word given.

1. Make **early** to mean *almost*. | _ e a r l y

2. Make **allow** to mean *not deep*. | _ _ a l l o w

3. Make **ram** into a metric measurement of weight. | _ r a m

4. Make **ales** into something for measuring weight. | _ _ a l e s

5. Make **old** to mean *bend part of something back*. | _ o l d

6. Make **ear** to mean *before the expected time*. | e a r _ _

7. Make **and** to mean *the pointers on a clock*. | _ a n d _

8. Make **ape** to mean *the outline of something*. | _ _ a p e

© Hopscotch: *Literacy Trios* ▲ Mathematical vocabulary

Name _____

Word games

▲ In this game you have to make a new word by adding another word to the one given. The first one is done for you.

1. Make BE mean *earlier in time*.   **B E F O R E**

2. Make SIDE mean *the outer surface of something*.

3. Make TERN mean *a layout of shapes obeying a rule*.

4. Make LID mean *no space inside*.

5. Make NIGHT mean *two weeks*.

6. Make SON mean *one of the four parts of the year*.

7. Make ACE mean *the outside covering of something*.

8. Make HIND mean *the other side of something*.

▲ Now make a new word by adding up to four letters to the word given.

1. Now make ATE go around and around.

2. Now make PEAT do it again and again.

3. Now make CAVE into a surface that curves inwards.

4. Now make GRAM into a drawing that explains something.

5. Now make LOW into an object with an empty inside.

6. Now make PART into leaving a place.

7. Now make EAR into arriving before the expected time.

8. Now make AMID into a feature found in Egypt.

Measures, shape and space

Name _____

Word games

Use a dictionary to help you with this activity.

▲ Select a beginning, a middle and an ending from the boxes below to make up the word that is the answer to the clue. Write this word in the appropriate answer box at the bottom of the page. Circle the word parts as you use them. Follow the example.

Beginnings	Middles	Endings
sphe pa hex cen af po oc per py (mea) tri equi per octa tra cal com pro	(sure) ri pen ag pe si en pass an ter tag ram lat trac ra he im tim	dicular id eter onal dar on cal es gle zium llel noon tor etre (ment) dron tion eral

1. Size, height or amount of something.

2. Distance around the outside of an area.

3. Instrument for drawing circles.

4. Metric measure of length.

5. List of days, weeks and months of the year.

6. Part of the day between morning and evening.

7. Ancient Egyptian burial tomb.

8. Shaped like a sphere.

9. 3-D shape that has eight faces.

10. 2-D shape with three sides.

11. Place taken by somebody or something.

12. Lines that are the same distance from each other along their full length.

13. Upright, at right angles to the horizontal.

14. Angle measurer.

15. Having all sides equal.

16. 2-D shape with eight sides.

17. Four-sided 2-D shape with one pair of parallel sides.

18. Having six straight sides.

1. *Measurement*	7.	13.
2.	8.	14.
3.	9.	15.
4.	10.	16.
5.	11.	17.
6.	12.	18.

© Hopscotch: *Literacy Trios* ▲ Mathematical vocabulary

Name _____

Homonyms

▲ Join the words in the ladders that have the same sound.
Then write each word carefully on the line at the side of the ladder.
The first one has been done for you.

week	week		wait	
	hour		tern	
	turn		our	
	time		knight	
	new		thyme	
	night		sloe	
	through		weak	*weak*
	slow		knew	
	weight		strait	
	straight		threw	

▲ Look up in a dictionary the meanings
of any words you don't know.

Name _____

Homonyms

▲ A homonym is a word with the same spelling or sound as another but with a different meaning. Join the meanings with the correct words. One has been done for you.

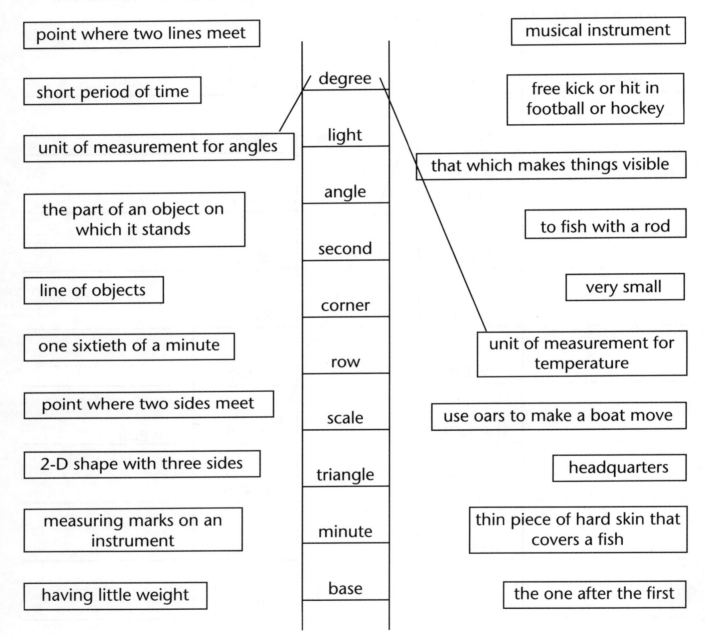

point where two lines meet		musical instrument
short period of time	degree	free kick or hit in football or hockey
unit of measurement for angles	light	that which makes things visible
the part of an object on which it stands	angle	to fish with a rod
line of objects	second	very small
one sixtieth of a minute	corner	unit of measurement for temperature
point where two sides meet	row	use oars to make a boat move
2-D shape with three sides	scale	headquarters
measuring marks on an instrument	triangle	thin piece of hard skin that covers a fish
having little weight	minute	the one after the first
	base	

▲ Use your dictionary to look up the exact meaning of five of the words on the ladder and write the word with its meaning on the back of this sheet.

© Hopscotch: *Literacy Trios* ▲ Mathematical vocabulary

Measures, shape and space

Homonyms

A homonym is a word with the same spelling or sound as another but with a different meaning.

▲ The words in the boxes have a mathematical meaning and, when used in a different context, at least one other meaning. Write down two definitions next to each word – one to show the mathematical meaning and the other to show an alternative. Use a dictionary to help you and make your definitions clear and concise.

plane	1. _____
	2. _____
pound	1. _____
	2. _____
obtuse	1. _____
	2. _____
degree	1. _____
	2. _____
reflect	1. _____
	2. _____
triangle	1. _____
	2. _____
division	1. _____
	2. _____
plan	1. _____
	2. _____
grid	1. _____
	2. _____
column	1. _____
	2. _____

Name _____

Choosing the right word

▲ Choose the correct word to write in each sentence.

lower
twice
hours
apart
Once

1. A _ _ _ _ _ _ _ _ edge has no _ _ _ _ _ _ in it.

2. There are sixty _ _ _ _ _ _ _ in one minute.

3. 20cm is _ _ _ _ _ _ than 10cm but _ _ _ _ _ _ _ than 40cm.

4. A _ _ _ _ _ _ _ _ _ and a _ _ _ _ _ _ both have four straight sides.

5. 30g is _ _ _ _ _ _ _ than 20g but _ _ _ _ _ _ _ than 50g.

straight
curves
seconds

minutes	heavier	square	rectangle

6. There are twenty-four _ _ _ _ _ in a day.

7. An hour has sixty _ _ _ _ _ _ _ .

8. The opposite of higher is _ _ _ _ _ _ .

9. When things are _ _ _ _ _ they are away from each other.

10. _ _ _ _ or _ _ _ _ _ a year I go skating at the ice rink.

longer
lighter
shorter

© Hopscotch: *Literacy Trios* ▲ Mathematical vocabulary

Name _____

Choosing the right word

▲ Choose the most suitable word to write in each sentence.

1. The line or course along which you move is called your _ _ _ _ _ _ _ _ _.

2. A _ _ _ _ _ _ _ _ _ _ is a very small volume of liquid.

3. The distance from the centre of a circle to the edge is the _ _ _ _ _ _.

4. A _ _ _ _ _ _ _ is an arrangement of numbers according to a rule.

5. An object is _ _ _ _ _ _ _ _ _ _ _ when it can be cut exactly in half.

6. A scale mark on a protractor is shown in _ _ _ _ _ _ _.

7. To _ _ _ _ _ _ means to turn.

degrees	perimeter	flat	cone	rotate
diagonal	corner	direction	radius	distance
millilitre	pattern	short	symmetrical	octagon

8. A two-dimensional shape is _ _ _ _.

9. A _ _ _ _ _ _ is a point where two lines meet.

10. An _ _ _ _ _ _ _ has eight sides.

11. A line across a shape from one corner to another is called a _ _ _ _ _ _ _ _.

12. A _ _ _ _ is a solid with a pointed top and a circular base.

13. The distance round a closed shape is the _ _ _ _ _ _ _ _ _.

14. The _ _ _ _ _ _ _ _ is the length of space between two places or things.

15. Something with not much length is _ _ _ _ _ _.

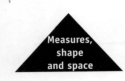

Choosing the right word

▲ Choose the most suitable word to write in each sentence.

1. An _____ angle is an angle of less than 90°.

2. If circles are _____ they have the same centre.

3. The _____ is the point where lines or edges meet.

4. A shape that is _____ is bent without angles.

5. An angle of 90° is called a _____ angle.

6. An eight-sided 2-D shape is called an _____ .

7. There are one thousand millilitres in a _____ .

8. An _____ angle is more than 90˚ but less than 180˚.

9. The _____ of a container is the amount that it will hold.

10. A _____ angle is more than 180 degrees but less than 360 degrees.

11. A _____ is a 3-D object with the shape of a circle along its length.

12. Lines or edges meet at _____ .

13. A line of _____ divides a 2-D shape so that one half is a mirror

    image of the other.

14. The radius of a circle is half the length of the _____ .

15. Lines running across a page the same distance apart are _____ .

16. The _____ is the distance around a circle.

17. If a triangle has two sides the same length it is an _____

    triangle.

18. A shape with sides and angles that are not equal is an _____

    shape.

19. A _____ line goes across a shape from one corner to another.

20. The border where an object begins or ends is called the _____ .

| edge |
| vertex |
| parallel |
| octagon |
| right |
| litre |
| reflex |
| acute |

obtuse	circumference	diagonal	concentric	capacity	symmetry
cylinder	isosceles	vertices	diameter	irregular	curved

© Hopscotch: *Literacy Trios* ▲ Mathematical vocabulary

Name _____

Secret codes

▲ Letters can be used to make secret codes. Study this alphabet code. The letters in the second row are the code.

A	B	C	D	E	F	G	H	I	J	K	L	M	N	O	P	Q	R	S	T	U	V	W	X	Y	Z
B	C	D	E	F	G	H	I	J	K	L	M	N	O	P	Q	R	S	T	U	V	W	X	Y	Z	A

Using this code UJNF spells TIME and MJUSF spells LITRE.

▲ Use the code to work out the words shown by these letters.

EBZ   IPVS   NJOVUF   TFDPOE

_____   _____   _____   _____

BVUVNO   TQSJOH   XJOUFS   TVNNFS

_____   _____   _____   _____

▲ Now do the same with each of these sentences.

JO GSPOU PG UIF IPVTF XBT B HBSEFO.

_____

CFIJOE UIF DVQCPBSE XBT B TQJEFS.

_____

Secret codes

Letters can be used to make secret codes. Study this alphabet code. The letters in the second row are the code.

A	B	C	D	E	F	G	H	I	J	K	L	M	N	O	P	Q	R	S	T	U	V	W	X	Y	Z
B	C	D	E	F	G	H	I	J	K	L	M	N	O	P	Q	R	S	T	U	V	W	X	Y	Z	A

Using this code TLFUDI spells SKETCH and DPODBWF spells CONCAVE.

▲ Use the code to work out the words shown by these letters.

EFHSFF   BTDFOE   CFUXFFO   JOTJEF   SFGMFDU

_____   _____   _____   _____   _____

QPMZHPO   SFDUBOHMF   DJSDMF   TQIFSF   DPOWFY

_____   _____   _____   _____   _____

▲ Now write this mathematical information using the secret code.

THE SURFACE IS THE OUTSIDE LAYER OF AN OBJECT.

_____

A COMPASS NEEDLE POINTS TOWARDS THE MAGNETIC NORTH.

_____

▲ On the back of this sheet write a message to a friend and ask them to decode it. Use the code at the top of the page or invent one of your own.

© Hopscotch: *Literacy Trios* ▲ Mathematical vocabulary

Name _____

Secret codes

A code is usually a system of letters or numbers used to keep messages secret.
Alphabet codes can be made by counting backwards or forwards one letter or more.
Number codes can be made by numbering the letters of the alphabet in any order.

▲ In a certain code the word PYRAMID is QZSBNJE. Fill in the remaining letters
of the code on the alphabet list below.

A	B	C	D	E	F	G	H	I	J	K	L	M	N	O	P	Q	R	S	T	U	V	W	X	Y	Z
B				F				J				N			Q			T						Z	

▲ Now use the code to write the meaning of:

DPODFOUSJD   NJMMJMJUSF   LJMPHSBN   QFSJNFUFS

_____   _____   _____   _____

B TFU TRVBSF JT BO JOTUSVNFOU GPS ESBXJOH PS GJOEJOH SJHIU BOHMFT.

_____

▲ Change these words and mathematical message into code.

ESTIMATE   APPROXIMATE   CIRCUMFERENCE   INTERSECTION

_____   _____   _____   _____

A CUBIC CENTIMETRE IS THE MOST COMMON UNIT OF VOLUME.

_____

▲ On a separate piece of paper write a message to a friend using the code below. Ask him
or her to decode it. Don't forget to let your friend have a copy of the decoding chart!
Instead, you could invent a code of your own and use that to send your message.

A	B	C	D	E	F	G	H	I	J	K	L	M	N	O	P	Q	R	S	T	U	V	W	X	Y	Z
1	Z	A	B	2	D	E	F	3	H	I	J	K	L	4	N	O	P	Q	R	5	T	U	V	W	X

Name _____

Data wordsearch

▲ In the wordsearch are eight words to do with handling data. Clues and first and last letters are given to help you. Search up, down and across and write the words on the lines when you find them. Some letters are used twice.

1. Put things in sets.

_____ s _ _ t _____

2. Number of people or things.

_____ g _ _ _ p _____

3. Lists of data in columns and rows.

_____ t _ _ _ e _____

4. Word that tells you what something means.

_____ l _ _ _ l _____

b	j	l	v	k	w	l	s
g	h	e	b	t	a	e	o
r	a	m	c	a	e	b	r
a	t	u	e	l	b	a	t
p	y	d	o	l	n	l	n
h	p	x	i	y	r	f	u
h	t	s	a	e	l	g	o
g	r	o	u	p	q	s	c

5. Diagram comparing things.

_____ g _ _ _ h _____

6. Say numbers in order.

_____ c _ _ _ t _____

7. Record of a score.

_____ t _ _ _ y _____

8. Smallest in size or amount.

_____ l _ _ _ t _____

▲ Colour green all the letters you have used on the wordsearch. Colour yellow all the letters you have not used.

© Hopscotch: *Literacy Trios* ▲ Mathematical vocabulary

Name _____

Data wordsearch

89

▲ In this wordsearch are ten words all to do with data handling. Find the words and write them down in the spaces provided. Some letters for each word are given as a clue. You will have to search in all directions except diagonally.

M	A	R	G	O	T	C	I	P
A	X	E	S	E	A	H	A	F
S	C	P	C	O	U	N	T	P
U	T	R	A	H	C	R	A	B
R	S	E	M	A	N	Y	D	K
V	U	S	D	P	A	E	H	C
E	M	E	L	B	A	T	A	C
Y	C	N	E	U	Q	E	R	F
B	I	T	R	O	S	A	E	G

1. P _ C _ _ _ _ _ M
2. R _ P _ _ S _ _ _
3. F R _ _ _ _ _ _ Y
4. A _ _ S
5. B _ _ C _ _ _ T
6. S _ _ V _ _
7. D _ _ _
8. C _ _ _ _
9. T _ _ _ _
10. S _ _ _

▲ Colour red all the letters you have used on the wordsearch.
Colour blue all the letters you have not used.

▲ Write down any other words you can find written on the wordsearch.
You may search for the words in all directions including diagonally.

_____

_____

_____

Handling data

Data wordsearch

▲ Hidden in this wordsearch are 14 words connected with data handling. Clues and first letters are given to help you find each one. Write down each word when you find it and shade it in on the wordsearch. You will have to search in all directions.

1. Collection of organised information.   D

   _____

2. The rate of occurrence of something.   F

   _____

3. The most frequent value in a set of data.   M

   _____

4. Facts and data based on numbers.   S

   _____

5. To arrange systematically in groups.   C

   _____

6. The result or effect of an event.   O

   _____

D	Z	B	D	T	T	N	U	O	C	S	D
Y	A	X	A	Y	A	D	L	S	S	I	I
E	W	T	T	S	F	L	V	E	H	X	A
B	M	U	A	R	A	I	L	I	S	T	G
A	O	O	R	B	E	B	S	Y	S	H	R
R	N	F	C	M	A	F	T	S	E	X	A
C	E	Q	O	T	Y	S	E	G	A	C	M
H	Y	C	N	E	U	Q	E	R	F	L	I
A	D	M	V	E	P	O	D	N	O	L	C
R	K	R	M	A	R	G	O	T	C	I	P
T	U	N	I	T	R	E	M	M	I	S	A
S	C	I	T	S	I	T	A	T	S	J	Y

7. A drawing that explains something.   D

   _____

8. A list of data in columns and rows.   T

   _____

9. To examine a subject by asking questions.   S

   _____

10. A graph with facts shown in picture form.   P

    _____

11. Information shown in columns.   B C

    _____

12. To say numbers in order.   C

    _____

13. The vertical and horizontal reference lines on a graph.   A

    _____

14. Record of a score.   T

    _____

▲ Write down any other words you can find in the wordsearch.

_____

_____

© Hopscotch: *Literacy Trios* ▲ Mathematical vocabulary

Name _____

Sentence construction

▲ Link words from each block to form a sentence.
One has been done for you.
Then carefully write out each sentence.

A <u>set</u> is	the name for	size or amount.
<u>Most</u> means	to put things	or figures.
To <u>sort</u> is	a record of	something.
A <u>list</u> shows	a group of things	in groups.
A <u>tally</u> is	greatest in	a score.
A <u>title</u> is	written words	that go together.

1. _____

2. _____

3. _____

4. *A list shows written words or figures.* _____

5. _____

6. _____

▲ On the back of this sheet put three of the underlined words into
separate sentences to show their meaning, like this example.

Before leaving for town, Mum looked for her shopping <u>list</u>.

Name _____

Sentence construction

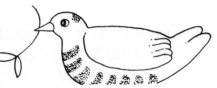

▲ Link words from each block to form a sentence. One has been done for you Write out each sentence. Don't forget to use capital letters and full stops.

<u>Data</u> is facts or information	to say or name	in written form.
To <u>survey</u> is to	show what you want	by asking questions.
The <u>frequency</u> of an event	that can be used	asking about people's opinions.
		it happens.
To <u>count</u> is	words or figures	numbers and amounts
To <u>vote</u> is to	examine a subject	compare.
		from a group of choices.
A <u>questionnaire</u> is	showing how	for deciding something.
A <u>graph</u> is a diagram	a list of questions	numbers in order.
A <u>list</u> shows	is how often	

1. _____

2. _____

3. _____

4. _____

5. _____

6. _____

7. *A graph is a diagram showing how numbers and amounts compare.*

8. _____

▲ On the back of this sheet put four of the underlined words into separate sentences to show their meaning.

© Hopscotch: *Literacy Trios* ▲ Mathematical vocabulary

Sentence construction

▲ Link words from each block to form a sentence. One has been done for you.
Write out each sentence. Don't forget to punctuate each one correctly.

The <u>axes</u> are the	examined by asking either written	organised information.
A <u>probable</u> event	a list of questions	of an event or action.
<u>Statistics</u> involves collecting	is a collection of	plan or intention.
The <u>frequency</u> is	the most frequent result	reference lines on a graph.
To <u>classify</u> information	happen without	based on a number of things.
In a <u>survey</u> a subject is	is likely to	in a set of data.
A <u>questionnaire</u> is	the rate of occurrence	happen.
The <u>mode</u> is	vertical and horizontal	in groups.
A <u>database</u>	is to arrange it systematically	or oral questions.
Things that happen by <u>chance</u>	classifying and interpreting information	asking about people's opinions.

1. _____

2. _____

3. _____

   _____

4. ___ *The frequency is the rate of occurrence of an event or action.* ___

5. _____

6. _____

   _____

7. _____

8. _____

9. _____

10. _____

▲ On the back of this sheet put five of the underlined words into separate
sentences to show their meaning.

Page 6
1. 1005 2. 1500 3. 1050 4. 20 006 5. 20 060
6. 26 000 7. 20 600 8. 300 008 9. 308 000
10. 300 800 11. 380 000 12. 300 080 13. 1 000 000
14. 1 700 000 15. 1 000 700 16. 1 000 007

1. Four thousand, eight hundred and sixty-five
2. Twenty-one thousand, three hundred and seventy-nine
3. Sixty thousand, five hundred and two
4. Fifty-one thousand and eight

Page 12 (last activity)
sequence, hundred, complete, symbol, incorrect, predict, compare, discuss

Page 14 (last activity)
Ten multiplied by ten equals one hundred.

Page 15
1. c, a, d, b 2. d, b, c, a 3. a, d, c, e, b 4. c, a, d, b

another way of writing a fraction or decimal
to change one thing for another
following continuously in unbroken order
a quality or characteristic of something

A sequence is a set of things that belong next to each other in a particular order. To classify items is to arrange them systematically into groups. A numeral is a symbol that represents a certain number.

Page 16 (last activity)
1. 50 2. 100 3. 10 4. 16 5. 56 6. 42

Page 17
1. no 2. no 3. no 4. no 5. yes
1. 66 2. 40 3. open ended 4. 5 5. 8

Page 18
1. 36 2. 75% 3. open ended 4. $\frac{1}{2}$ $\frac{4}{5}$ $\frac{2}{3}$ (circled)
5. 4.7 6. six-fifths, nine-sixths, nine-thirds (ringed)
7. open ended 8. 125
1. 143 2. 353 3. 582 4. 24 5. 6809 6. 1249 7. 741

Page 21
greatest, smallest, before, between, estimate, exactly, nearest, positive, negative, pattern, investigate, justify

Page 22
Zero, Digit, More, Large, Small, Before, Nearly, Over, Under, Guess

Page 23
Predict, Exchange, Order, Estimate, Exactly, Numeral, Subtract, Classify, Approximate, Great, Many, Compare

Page 24
NOTHING, NIL   NUMEROUS, PROFUSE
VAST, BIG   BEHIND, LATER
VIRTUALLY, ROUGHLY   ABSOLUTELY, FAULTLESSLY
RELATIONSHIP, SIMILARITY   CATEGORISE, ARRANGE
PECULIARITY, PROPERTY   PLENTY, SUFFICIENT

Page 25
1. 4 2. 7 3. 150 4. 2 5. 6 6. 17 7. 8

1. twenty 2. five 3. fifteen 4. nine 5. three
6. twenty-four

Page 26
1. 1 2. 40 3. 30 4. 16

1. column 2. row 3. once 4. twice 5. subtract
6. half

Page 27
1. 2 2. 161 3. 270 4. 180 5. 20 6. 24

twenty, nineteen   twenty-five, thirty

Page 31
ACROSS – 1. 23 4. 24   DOWN – 2. 31 3. 14
ACROSS – 1. 76 4. 23   DOWN – 2. 62 3. 22

Page 32
ACROSS – 1. 55 2. 979 3. 82 4. 213
DOWN – 1. 592 2. 93 3. 83 5. 12
ACROSS – 1. 997 3. 741 5. 40 7. 12
DOWN – 2. 779 4. 142 6. 7

Page 33
ACROSS – 1. 34 830 5. 49 6. 887 7. 525 9. 93
10. 2025 12. 973 13. 44 14. 12
DOWN – 2. 46 3. 31 815 4. 6953 8. 55 9. 9173
10. 26 11. 224

Page 35 (second activity)
1. How many are left when...27 2. How many more than... 34 3. What is the total of... 95

Page 36
B, E, D, A, C

Page 40
1. Penny 2. Change 3. Cheap 4. Spend 5. Price
6. Money 7. Cost 8. Bought

Page 41
1. Value 2. Expensive 3. Change 4. Pence 5. Spend
6. Bought 7. Sold 8. Amount 9. Pay 10. Pound

Page 42
1. Banknote 2. Capital 3. Cheque 4. Currency
5. Loss 6. Profit 7. Expensive 8. Value 9. Bought
10. Sell 11. Coin 12. Cost 13. Spend 14. Cheap

Page 43
right, wrong, correct, sign, pattern, puzzle

coin, pound, spend, change

Page 44
answer, method, calculate, jotting, symbol, puzzle, pattern, correct, wrong

note, penny, bought, expensive, cheap

Page 45
1. pattern 2. calculation 3. profit 4. discount
5. value 6. loss

symbol, equation, method, expensive, calculate

Page 48
tomorrow, calendar, fortnight, today, millennium, weekend, yesterday, century, always, never

1. SECONDS, MINUTES 2. ANALOGUE 3. DAY, HOURS 4. QUARTER 5. DIGITAL, DISPLAY 6. HALF

Page 52
1. circle 2. pentagon 3. hexagon 4. triangle
5. rectangle 6. square

1. cube 2. sphere 3. cylinder 4. cone

Page 53
1. cube 2. circle 3. hexagon 4. rectangle 5. prism
6. sphere 7. pentagon 8. cylinder 9. square
10. polygon 11. cuboid 12. octagon 13. cone
14. triangle

Page 54
1. triangle 2. octagon 3. semicircle 4. cube
5. polyhedron 6. rhombus 7. cone 8. pentagon
9. octahedron 10. circle 11. cylinder 12. hexagon
13. pyramid 14. rectangle 15. square 16. cuboid
17. polygon 18. sphere 19. tetrahedron
20. hemisphere

Page 55
Under, Inside, Bottom, Back, Right, Below, Down, After, Higher, Forwards

Page 56
Edge, Lower, Backwards, Outside, Column, Anticlockwise, South, West, Vertical, Front, Before

Page 57
OVER, ABOVE, TOP, INSIDE, BACK, AFTER, CENTRE, LEFT, UP, HIGHER, FORWARDS, FAR, ASCEND, ROW, CLOCKWISE, NORTH, EAST, HORIZONTAL, SMALLER, LONGITUDE

Page 60
gallon, kilogram, distance, empty, balance, centimetre, centilitre, kilometre, millilitre, heaviest, shallow, ounce

1. An approximate amount is one that is almost exact but not completely so.
2. A millimetre is equivalent to one thousandth of a metre.
3. Miles, yards, feet and inches are all imperial measurements of length.
4. Tonnes, kilograms and grams are all metric measurements of mass.

Page 64
ACROSS – 1. depth 4. year 6. metre 7. Tues
10. edge
DOWN – 1. day 2. playtime 3. he 5. left 6. month
8. 3-D 9. 2-D

Page 65
ACROSS – 1. many 3. am 6. surface 7. low
9. draw 12. little 14. third
DOWN – 1. measure 2. nearly 4. more 5. shallow
8. wide 10. after 11. flat 13. pm

Page 66
ACROSS – 1. estimate 6. inside 7. net 8. cube
11. radius 12. low 13. light 15. over 18. shallow
DOWN – 1. equilateral 2. Tuesday 3. middle 4. top
5. centre 9. before 10. night 14. inch 16. roll
17. old

Page 76
1. WEEKEND 2. BEDTIME 3. ACROSS 4. SIDEWAYS
5. BESIDE 6. SOMETIMES

1. NEARLY 2. SHALLOW 3. GRAM 4. SCALES
5. FOLD 6. EARLY 7. HANDS 8. SHAPE

Page 77
1. BEFORE 2. OUTSIDE 3. PATTERN 4. SOLID
5. FORTNIGHT 6. SEASON 7. SURFACE 8. BEHIND

1. ROTATE 2. REPEAT 3. CONCAVE 4. DIAGRAM
5. HOLLOW 6. DEPART 7. EARLY 8. PYRAMID

Page 78
1. measurement 2. perimeter 3. compasses
4. centimetre 5. calendar 6. afternoon 7. pyramid
8. spherical 9. octahedron 10. triangle 11. position
12. parallel 13. perpendicular 14. protractor
15. equilateral 16. octagon 17. trapezium
18. hexagonal

Page 82
1. straight, curves 2. seconds 3. longer, shorter
4. rectangle, square 5. heavier, lighter 6. hours
7. minutes 8. lower 9. apart 10. Once, twice

Page 83
1. direction 2. millilitre 3. radius 4. pattern
5. symmetrical 6. degrees 7. rotate 8. flat 9. corner
10. octagon 11. diagonal 12. cone 13. perimeter
14. distance 15. short

Page 84
1. acute 2. concentric 3. vertex 4. curved 5. right
6. octagon 7. litre 8. obtuse 9. capacity 10. reflex
11. cylinder 12. vertices 13. symmetry 14. diameter
15. parallel 16. circumference 17. isosceles
18. irregular 19. diagonal 20. edge

Page 85
DAY, HOUR, MINUTE, SECOND, AUTUMN, SPRING,
WINTER, SUMMER

IN FRONT OF THE HOUSE WAS A GARDEN.
BEHIND THE CUPBOARD WAS A SPIDER.

Page 86
DEGREE, ASCEND, BETWEEN, INSIDE, REFLECT,
POLYGON, RECTANGLE, CIRCLE, SPHERE, CONVEX

UIF TVSGBDF JT UIF PVUJEF MBZFS PG BO
PCKFDU.
B DPNQBTT OFFEMF QPJOUT UPXBSET UIF
NBHOFUJD OPSUI.

Page 87
CONCENTRIC, MILLILITRE, KILOGRAM, PERIMETER

A SET SQUARE IS AN INSTRUMENT FOR DRAWING
OR FINDING RIGHT ANGLES.

FTUJNBUF BQQSPYJNBUF DJSDVNGFSFODF
JOUFSTFDUJPO

B DVCJD DFOUJNFUSF JT UIF NPTU DPNNPO
VOJU PG WPMVNF.

Page 88
1. sort 2. group 3. table 4. label 5. graph
6. count 7. tally 8. least

Page 89
1. Pictogram 2. Represent 3. Frequency 4. Axes
5. Bar Chart 6. Survey 7. Data 8. Count 9. Table
10. Sort

Page 90
1. Database 2. Frequency 3. Mode 4. Statistics
5. Classify 6. Outcome 7. Diagram 8. Table
9. Survey 10. Pictogram 11. Bar Chart 12. Count
13. Axes 14. Tally